NEAR EASTERN MYTHOLOGY

NEAR EASTER

John Gray

Hamlyn

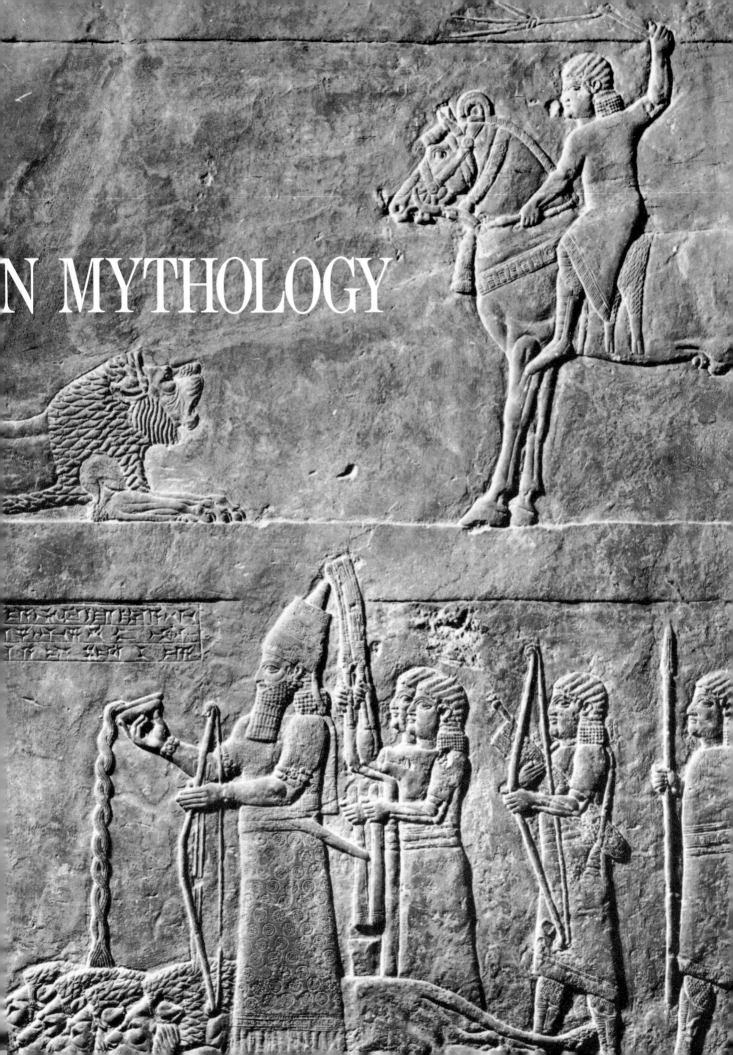

N MYTHOLOGY

The Hamlyn Publishing Group Limited
London New York Sydney Toronto
Hamlyn House, Feltham, Middlesex, England
SBN: 600 036 383
Copyright © John Gray 1969
All rights reserved
Filmset by Filmtype Services, Scarborough
Printed in Italy by O.G.A.M. Verona
Extracts from *Ancient Near Eastern texts
relating to the Old Testament*, edited by
James B. Pritchard, Princeton University
Press, rev. edn. 1955, reprinted by
permission of Princeton University Press.
Extracts from *The legacy of Canaan*, by
John Gray, 1965, reprinted by permission
of E. J. Brill, Leiden.

Contents

ISREAL

Colour Plates

MESOPOTAMIA

'History', it has been said, 'begins at Sumer'. This is perhaps a somewhat misleading statement in view of the contemporary and independent civilisations in Egypt and the Indus Valley, to say nothing of the basic achievements of earlier agricultural communities three or four millennia before the Sumerian settlement in South Mesopotamia. But it rightly emphasises the main impetus to man's understanding of his environment and co-operation for its control in Mesopotamia.

THE SUMERIANS

There, where the capricious floods of the Tigris and Euphrates deposited their enormous load of silt owing to the natural filter of the extensive marshes, the rich alluvial plain lay at the mercy of baking sun and flood waters. It awaited masters with the political organisation to irrigate and to drain to bring Order out of watery Chaos. This antithesis can still be seen today in the curious amphibious world of the marshes, where man still wins land from water, often with his naked hands. This immemorial struggle, we shall find, is the theme of the liturgy of the New Year festival in Babylonia and Assyria. The periodic great flood is as real a tradition in modern times as among the ancient Sumerians, who regarded the legendary flood as the 'great divide' between history and pre-history. For them the earliest period was punctuated not by individual reigns, but by dynasties, their founders and their most conspicuous rulers. As a result, the Sumerian king-lists give the impression of patriarchs in comparison with whom Methuselah was a mere youth.

Here in the south we find the first articulate evidence of man's relation with his environment in Sumerian mythology. Towards the middle of the fourth millenium B.C. men evolved writing with a sharp stylus on damp clay. They used simple pictorial signs, which were at first stylised to express words and then developed to spell out the combinations of consonants and primary vowels as syllables. This development was a by-product of the growth of communities round temples, divine estates in fact, where accounts were meticulously kept. In such communities, where both the inhabitants and the natural resources of the divine estate were organised to form city states, men first strove towards a systematic understanding of their environment.

It is too early even in the third millenium B.C. to expect detached philosophy. The ancient Mesopotamian was too much involved in his environment. Eventually in a more humanistic age, which is beyond the scope of this study, he was capable of observing and classifying natural phenomena, although he never displayed complete objectivity, because in his classification he had the practical purpose of adjusting society more harmoniously to the larger environment in which it was involved. In the myths that we shall study there is some tendency towards a scientific approach, but the dramatic representation betrays emotional involvement which is not scientific. We shall notice many elements which contradict logic in Near Eastern mythology. This is especially true of ritual, where time-honoured and important cult practices have left their traces in the myths. In a just appreciation of Mesopotamian mythology this must be remembered. It is equally important to recognise that most of the myths we shall consider are the result of long elaboration, even if they achieved their extant literary form in the third millenium, and that they are the exercise of the scientific mind of the times.

Historical geography

Above: a silver model of a *tarada*, or boat, from the royal tombs of Ur (*c.* 2900 B.C.). It is of a similar pattern to the boat in a marsh village in southern Mesopotamia shown on the preceding page.

The origin of the Sumerians, a broad-headed people, who were physically and linguistically quite different from the Semites, is one of the great unsolved problems of history. It has been conjectured that they came from the south-east, either by way of southern Persia or by the Persian Gulf. Their early familiarity with ships seems to support the latter view, and it is perhaps significant that the scene of one of their myths is laid in Tilmun, which has been identified with the island of Bahrein in the Persian Gulf. The myth concerns the origin and development of agriculture and its by-products in a conflict between Ninhursag the Earth-mother and Enki, the waters both sinister and beneficent. Further support of this provenance of the Sumerians may be found in the myth of Oannes. According to this myth Oannes, a being half fish and half human, issued from the sea to teach men writing, science, the arts, the building of cities and temples, agriculture and the amenities of life, all in fact that was distinctive of Sumerian culture, and disappeared each night under the waters. This, it is true, may simply be a version of the Sumerian tradition which regarded Ea the god of water as also the god of wisdom. Certainly Oannes seems a likely version of Ea. Nevertheless, the tradition of civilisation emerging fully developed without the long, painful process of evolution agrees with the sudden urban settlement of southern Mesopotamia by a people from overseas who brought with them the necessary skills and political organisation to control land and water in such a region.

Here then the Sumerians built cities around their temples on the alluvial plain round the marshes, cultivated cereals and dates, for which the land is famous, and bred cattle. They also built ships for navigation from the canals and lagoons to the Tigris and Euphrates rivers and to the Persian Gulf, and sent caravans to the highlands of Iran, to Asia Minor, to Syria, and, early in the third millennium B.C., even to Egypt and the Indus Valley. The metals and stones of the distant mountains were prized in this alluvial land, and the cedars of Lebanon and Amanus were also coveted. In the Gilgamesh legend there is a tradition of a garden in the distant northern mountains, the fruits of which were precious stones. The importance of cedars is shown in the exploit of Gilgamesh and his companion Enkidu against the giant of the cedar forest.

The Sumerians developed autonomous city states, which with their land and all their technical, commercial and intellectual enterprises were organised as great temple-estates. H. Frankfort has termed the system 'theocratic communism', where the priest of the chief god of the city was the tenant-farmer, or steward (Sumerian *ensi*). On occasion a single ruler, or 'great man' (Sumerian *lugal*), might be appointed in emergency, like the dictator in the Roman republic, and a royal dynasty might be founded. This political development is reflected in the myth from the liturgy of the Babylonian New Year festival, where the great gods in council being at a loss to meet the menace to order from the inert waters, Marduk, the city-god of Babylon (and evidently in an earlier version of the myth Enlil, the storm god and executive of the heavenly court) undertakes the struggle, for which he is invested with the kingship. The ruler, however, was always regarded as the human executive of the divine king, the chief god of the city, a conception which persisted in Mesopotamia, Syria and Palestine, where it is most familiar in the Old Testament in Psalms 2 and 110. The potential evils of monarchy clearly

Below: a cane-plaited guest and council hall in a marsh village in southern Mesopotamia in the flood season.

emerge in the Legend of Gilgamesh 'two thirds god and one third man': the prelude to his heroic exploits was tyranny at home.

THE DESERT TRIBESMEN

Southern Mesopotamia flourished under the intensive administration and cultivation of the rulers of the Sumerian city-states. Other peoples from beyond the land of the two rivers, the Semites from the steppes of north-eastern Arabia and the highlanders from the Iranian plateau to the east, came into the country. The former were known as herdsmen and probably also as conductors of ass-caravans for the Sumerian merchants, travelling northwards along the desert edge, where their tribal connections were the safest insurance for the goods they carried.

The Semites of the steppes had seasonal grazing rights in the settled land after harvest, as they still have in the Near East. This is recognised in an ancient Sumerian myth where the shepherd Dumuzi and the farmer Enkidu sue for the hand of Inanna the queen of heaven. The sun-god Uttu, the brother of the goddess, presses the suit of the shepherd, recommending his butter and his milk. Nevertheless, Inanna prefers the more sophisticated clothes the farmer can provide, and his beans and grain to the precarious living of the shepherd. The rejected shepherd soothes his wounded pride by matching the farmer's assets with his own, the farmer's dressed cloth with his own woollen stuff, the farmer's beer with his 'yellow milk', the farmer's beans with his own cheese, the farmer's bread with his own honey. Eventually Inanna and her farmer-husband allow seasonal grazing rights to the shepherd, declaring:

I against thee, O shepherd, against thee, O shepherd, I against thee
Why shall I strive?
Let thy sheep eat the grass of the riverbank,
In my meadowland let thy sheep walk about,
In the bright fields of Erech let them eat grain,
Let thy kids and thy lambs drink the water of my Unun canal.

This text may have left a trace in the Biblical story of Cain the farmer and Abel the shepherd (Genesis 4, 2 ff). This story is favourable to the shepherd Abel, although he is the sufferer. The myth is also adapted in Hebrew tradition where Cain is not only a farmer, but a nomad smith. This detail probably reflects its adaptation and currency among nomad smith clans who roamed the Fertile Crescent between Mesopotamia and Syria along the desert edge.

But the hungry tribesmen were also a menace to security in the settled land, as was notably demonstrated in the great Arab raids which culminated in the Muslim conquest of Iraq after the death of Muhammad. The desert in consequence was an uncanny place to the people of the settled land. They saw it as the region of insecurity, the unpredictable, from which came wild men, raiding and wrecking, and destructive hot winds and dust-storms. In Mesopotamian mythology it was, therefore, the preserve of the sinister supernatural powers, the malevolent demons, who were legion to the ancient Mesopotamian. So the Semites of the desert, with whom for better or worse the Sumerians were in constant contact, were powers to be conciliated. This situation is reflected in the Gilgamesh Legend, where the first antagonist worthy of the redoubtable King of Uruk (Biblical Erech) was Enkidu, the

Top: gypsum drinking trough (*c.* 3000 B.C.) with low reliefs of animals and lambs running from reed huts, such as are still in use in the marshes of southern Mesopotamia. The loop-headed symbol is that of the fertility-goddess Innana, or Ishtar, with whose temple the sculpture was possibly associated. British Museum.

Centre: limestone votive plaque from Tello (*c.* 2630 B.C.) of Urnanshi of Lagash, the 'great man', or 'steward of the god', depicted in the important role of temple-builder, carrying a basket of mud-bricks. The status of the king in ancient Mesopotamia is indicated by the proportion in which he is scaled relatively to his associates, the heir-apparent Akurgal, who stands next to him, and his retainers, all of whom are named. Louvre.

Bottom: stele commemorating a victory of Naram-sin of Akkad (2159-2133 B.C.), who is depicted larger than his followers and with the horns of divinity. Louvre.

wild man of the steppe, who after a tremendous combat worthy of both heroes became the companion of Gilgamesh on his various adventures.

The enemies from the east, the highlanders from the Iranian escarpment and plateau, were more formidable foes. They did not come into contact with the Sumerians regularly enough for the two peoples to live in peace. They were powers foreign in race and culture and, unlike the Bedouin from the North Arabian steppes, organised for campaigns. At various times they brought down ruling dynasties and laid the city-states in ruin. They were one of the constant menaces that beset life in Mesopotamia, where, unlike Egypt in the security of the Nile valley, men were conscious of the sinister potential of the forces of history and nature. Both these forces in Mesopotamian religion were expressions of the violence of Enlil the storm god, who was both destroyer and preserver. Thus a lament on the ruin of Ur attributes the destruction to Enlil.

SEMITIC DOMINATION

It was to be expected that at some point in the history of Mesopotamia the virile Semitic element in the population which had settled and assimilated the culture of the Sumerians should aspire to dominate. Such domination was won by the Semitic power in the city of Agade, or Akkad, under Sargon, the first really great imperialist in history (2242–2186). Sargon's policies were continued by his grandson Naram-sin (2159–2123). This Akkadian hegemony in southern Mesopotamia was not sustained, and there was a reversion to Sumerian hegemony under the Third Dynasty of Ur (2044–1936). But in the Akkadian ascendancy the Sumerian syllabic cuneiform signs were adapted to the writing of Semitic dialects in what is known as Akkadian. This was used by the Semitic Amorites from the western steppes, who next dominated Mesopotamia (1826–1526) and of whom the most familiar figure is Hammurabi (1724–1682).

Though the Semites made their own distinctive contribution to culture, religion, politics and literature, they also assimilated the substantial heritage of the Sumerians, often with little adaptation. Thus, while the mythology of Mesopotamia is really Sumerian, it was appropriated by the Semites in southern Mesopotamia in the older Akkadian period or in the later Amorite period. Sumerian mythology was also taken over to a certain degree by the Assyrians in northern Mesopotamia from about 1200 B.C. until the fall of the Assyrian empire with the destruction of Nineveh in 612 B.C. In fact, the literary sources for our information about Mesopotamian mythology are mainly copies of older Sumerian and Akkadian versions from temples in southern Mesopotamia collected and copied by the order of the Assyrian King Ashurbanipal (668-626) and deposited in his library of tablets.

The native tradition of Mesopotamia continued to flourish for almost another century after the fall of Nineveh, when another Semitic power, the Aramaeans, usually called Chaldaeans, from the western steppes came to power in Babylon. They dominated the country until they too fell to the ascendant power of the Persians under Cyrus the Great, who captured Babylon in 538 B.C. The Persians had their own mythology, or rather their own conception of the natural and supernatural order, formulated by the religion of Zoroaster. This cosmic philosophy, influenced by Babylonian astronomy, had an effect on late Jewish thought and Messianic expectation.

Boundary-stone (*kudurru*) with adjurations by the great gods represented by the heavenly bodies and by minor local deities represented by animals. The latter were considered to be potent local guarantors, like the *welis*, or local patron-spirits, among the Arabs. British Museum.

Religion

The first thing that impresses us is the extraordinarily animated world in which men in ancient Mesopotamia lived. On the level of popular daily religion, as illustrated by a multitude of incantations and counter-incantations, they felt themselves surrounded by a host of supernatural forces, both beneficial and malicious. Daily mishaps, headaches, toothache and even neighbours' quarrels were attributed to their appropriate demons, many of which, though identified with those disorders, were unnamed and located in the desert on the western horizon. Others might be more particularly personified, such as Namtar of Ashakku, the demon of plague or wasting disease, depicted in Psalm 41 as stalking the streets like 'the pestilence that walketh in darkness'. Nightmares and other nocturnal fears and menaces were the activity of *lilitu* (the 'night-hag'), *lilith* of Isiah 34. The sin that would 'lurk' (Hebrew *robhes*, literally 'couching') at the door of the fratricide Cain (Genesis 4.7) is an interesting survival of such a belief in Israel, *rabisu* being a Mesopotamian demon active in nightmares.

ANU AND ENLIL

On a higher level the official religion of the city-states was not substantially different. The all-embracing sky above in its infinitude, from which the sun shone and the rain fell, was deified as Anu, the supreme king and the source of order and government in the natural and supernatural worlds. Human kingship, often indeed called *anitu* ('Anu-ship'), is stated in royal texts to have come down from Anu.

The wind, which might dry up the flood waters of the Tigris and the Euphrates after they had overflowed the fields in spring and early summer, or bring rain to grazing grounds beyond the flood area, or fill the sails of vessels in the rivers or canals, or fertilise the blossoms of the rich palm-groves, thereby securing order in nature and society, was worshipped as Enlil. He was also a king, the god personally involved in the struggle with suffering in the world, as Anu was the divine sovereign, the heavenly repository of final authority. Enlil, as the executive of Anu, was more particularly the prototype of the human king as the active upholder of the royal authority which he derived from Anu and of the order for which that authority stood. As 'the able man', to follow Thomas Carlyle's etymology, the king's power was often described as *enlilitu* ('Enlil-ship'). But the Mesopotamian was realist enough to know that in a land exposed to the capricious floods of the Tigris and Euphrates, to the dust-storms and simooms (hot parching winds) of the desert, to locust-swarms which came drifting in on the wind from the western desert, to marauding Bedouin or wild highland invaders from Iran, he might expect calamity as well as benefit from the executive of royal Anu and the divine council. So Enlil was known in the destructive storm and even, as at the downfall of Ur, in the ruin wreaked by hostile armies.

ENKI, GOD OF WATER

The earth was regarded as a living deity Ninhursag ('Lady Mountain'), expressive of the building up of silt above the marshes and flood-waters of lower Mesopotamia. An ancient myth explains the origin of vegetation from the union of Ninhursag with Enki, also called Ea, the god of the waters. The myth, describing the generation of agriculture and its by-products from the initial union of Enki and Ninhursag and the consequent infidelities of Enki with his own daughters, opens with the following remarkable passage:

Top: Babylonian seal-impression of the fertility-gods. The naked Ishtar stands on a fire-breathing lion-monster, which is yoked to the chariot of the storm-god Enlil, or Adad. The scene recalls 'the Bitch of the gods Fire', one of the monsters of Chaos subdued by the fertility-gods Anat and Baal-Hadad in the Ras Shamra texts. Pierpont Morgan Library, New York.

Bottom: seal-impression (c. 990-660 B.C.) of 'the priest Nabunasir son of the priest of the god Adad', the fertility-god symbolised by the winged disc, whose function, stimulated by the fertility-genii with their fertilising bucket, is to provide rain. The central figure may be that of the priest in the attitude of worship. The strange position of the legs, if not occasioned by the inscription, may indicate an ecstatic dance like that of the dervishes of Baal on Mt. Carmel (1 Kings 18.26). British Museum.

The land Tilmun is pure, the land Tilmun is clean,
· · · · · ·
In Tilmun the raven utters no cries,
The *ittidu* bird utters not the cry of the *ittidu* bird,
The lion kills not,
The wolf snatches not the lamb,
Unknown is the kid-devouring wild dog,
· · · · · ·
The sick-eyed says not 'I am sick-eyed',
The sick-headed says not 'I am sick-headed',
Its old woman says not 'I am an old woman',
Its old man says not 'I am an old man',
· · · · · ·

This is a description of things 'in the beginning' before phenomena had acquired their characteristics. It is reminiscent of the description of first origins in Genesis (2.19–20) in which the various creatures are characterised by primeval man who gives them their respective names. The imagery of the old Sumerian myth seems to have found an echo in the moving vision of universal concord of which the king as God's executive in Israel is the guarantee (Isaiah 11.6–11):

The wolf will dwell with the lamb,
And the leopard lie down with the kid,
And the calf and the lion and the fatling together,
And a little child shall lead them. . . .

The myth of Enki and Ninhursag ends with Ninhursag cursing her fickle consort, the god of the waters, which is evidently a recognition of the fact that water really belongs to the dark underground. When the heavenly court objects, Ninhursag is persuaded to mitigate the curse, a recognition of the beneficial effect of water. It is interesting to find the recognition of tension as well as co-operation between the two forces of earth and water in the production and sustaining of life. The myth thus realistically reflects the physical conditions of life in southern Mesopotamia. Nothing so well illustrates the acute sense of the dynamic relationship of man and the necessities of life to the elemental forces of his environment as this myth of origins. It also, incidentally, illustrates the basic Mesopotamian belief in an order behind the tensions of nature, to which man must seek to adjust his life.

The god Enki, or Ea, the god of water, was also considered the supreme god of wisdom and magic, doubtless owing to the subtle pervasiveness of

Top: Shamash rises between the two mountains between hinged doors bounding the earth which are kept by divine guardians. British Museum.

Centre: Akkadian seal-impression (c. 2360-2180 B.C.) depicting Shamash the sun-god, with his saw, rising from the earth between the mountains of the East and the West between the fertility-goddess Ishtar with her lion and Ea the god of water. British Museum.

Bottom: Akkadian seal-impression (c. 2340-2180 B.C.) depicting the Zu-bird representing the forces of Chaos led before Ea by two gods, the second with a spear to the neck of the bird-man, and followed by a god carrying seven objects over his shoulder. These may represent the heads of the monster of Chaos, the seven-headed dragon. The significance of Ea in this context is either as god of potent spells or as judge. British Museum.

water both above and below the earth and to the vital part it plays in engendering life and thus making possible the development of vegetation and communications by the skill of man. This conception of water was also fostered by trial by ordeal. Suspects were thrown into the river, as witches used to be in Europe, to test their guilt or innocence according to whether they sank or floated. In legal texts which prescribe or record such trials, it is significant that the word 'river' is introduced by the initial cuneiform sign for 'god'. Enki had the power to impose or remove spells and curses. Connected with this power was the custom of concentrating the disabilities of the community in a sheep which was then slaughtered and thrown into the river. This practice was the Mesopotamian counterpart of the rite of the scapegoat in the religion of Israel in the Second Temple (Leviticus 16.1−28).

To list the vast number of gods great and small mentioned in Sumerian literature would be both tedious and confusing, though the list of the great gods of the elements might be reduced by recognising that the same deities appeared under various titles and that there was a considerable degree of coalescence of local deities reflecting political consolidation among the Sumerians. We shall avoid a tedious catalogue of gods and consider only the major deities.

SHAMASH, THE SUN-GOD

In the Babylon of Hammurabi's age, about 1700 B.C., one of the most active gods was Shamash, the sun, called also Babbar, perhaps a form of *barbar* 'the Bright One'. The sun had also been venerated by the Sumerians, particularly at Larsa and Sippar, where he was named Uttu. He was appropriately the enemy of darkness and all the evils which darkness anciently symbolised. He was 'the sun . . . with healing in his wings', who dispelled disease, and to the oppressed he was the vindicator. As the god who traverses the whole sky from horizon to horizon and even, according to Mesopotamian cosmology, accomplishes a similar nightly journey through the underworld, he sees all wrongs, both open and hidden, and is the great god of justice. He demands justice from the ruler and is the champion of his subjects, particularly the under-privileged. This characteristic is particularly well illustrated in the prologue to Hammurabi's famous code of laws and on the sculpture at the head of the code, where the king stands subserviently before Shamash, from whom he receives the symbols of his commission.

SIN, THE MOON-GOD

The moon-god Sin is well known in the Sumerian pantheon through the stimulating discoveries of the late Sir Leonard Woolley at Ur, Sin's chief cult-centre in southern Mesopotamia. The moon, marking as it does the regular passage of time, particularly impressed the ancients, and was the god chiefly venerated in the pre-Christian civilisation of southern Arabia. There was great interest in trade overseas and over the desert, where expeditions might take months and even years. Time reckoning was an important factor in provisioning an expedition and in estimating its duration and the period for which income would be suspended. This may possibly explain the supreme regard in which the moon-god was held. It is significant that the Semites of the great caravan city of Palmyra in the first three centuries of the Christian era also gave high priority to the worship of the moon (Yerakh or Yarkhibol). The high regard for the moon in Sumerian religion may point to the voyage of the Sumerian settlers, who evidently came in an organised expedition by the Persian Gulf, which would involve a reckoning of months. In view of what we have noticed of the cult of the moon in the mercantile states of southern Arabia and Palmyra, it is surely not a mere coincidence that, after Ur, the most important cult-centre of the moon-god in Mesopotamia was Harran in northern Mesopotamia, which actually means 'caravan'. There the mother of King Nabona'id, the last king of Babylon (556–539 B.C.), was a priestess of the moon-god.

From the Sumerian myth of the union of Enki and Ninhursag and from Enki's numerous female progeny, we may infer the significance of female deities, all variations of the mother-goddess, a central figure in all nature religions. This deity, generally called Inanna among the Sumerians, was identified among the Semitic Amorites and Assyrians with Ishtar.

INANNA OR ISHTAR, THE MOTHER-GODDESS

The natural interest of man in the increase of crop and flock and indeed of the family is reflected from the earliest times in Palaeolithic Europe in cave-paintings of pregnant females, and in Mesopotamia and Palestine by nude female figurines. The mother-goddess played a most important role in myth and ritual to stimulate the desired increase. The principle was that of homoeopathic or imitative magic, by which men influenced the gods by auto-suggestion in the form of their primitive prayers, and indicated the intensity of their involvement in the supernatural processes thus thought to be stimulated. The sacred marriage between god and goddess was an important rite in Sumerian religion and indeed in nature-religion among the Semites in the Near East in all periods and regions except in Israel. In Mesopotamia it is depicted on a cylinder seal from Tell Asmar from the middle of the second millennium B.C. and it is known from ritual texts that

Libation beaker with inscription of Gudea (c. 2275-2260 B.C.): 'divine steward of Lagash, who dedicated it to Ningizzidu his god, that his life may be lengthened'. Two winged dragons are depicted with serpent head and the horned crown of divinity and holding each a ringed post, or doorpost. Under the spout two serpents are represented coiled round a staff, like the symbol of the classical healing-god Asclepius. The serpent, owing to its annual renewal of its skin, was the symbol of life and rejuvenation. Louvre.

in the city of Isin about the end of the third millennium B.C. the sacred marriage was annually enacted by the king as representative of the vegetation-god Tammuz and a priestess representing Inanna.

The mother-goddess Inanna, to whom the Semitic Ishtar was assimilated, was thus the channel of fertility to men, the great lover and mother. Her love was insatiable, consuming and even fatal, as indicated in a passage in the Gilgamesh Legend:

Which lover didst thou love forever?
Which of thy shepherds pleased thee for all time?
· · · · · · ·
For Tammuz, the lover of thy youth,
Thou hast ordained wailing year after year,
Having loved the dappled shepherd-bird,
Thou smotest him, breaking his wing.
In the groves he sits, crying *kappi* (my wing!)
Then thou didst love a lion, perfect in strength;
Seven pits and seven thou didst dig for him.
Then a stallion thou lovedst, famed in battle;
The whip, the spur and the lash thou ordainedst for him.
Thou decreedst for him to gallop seven leagues,
Thou decreedst for him the muddied water to drink
... Then thou lovedst the keeper of the herd,
Who ash-cakes ever did heap up for thee,
Daily slaughtering kids for thee;
Yet thou smotest him, turning him into a wolf,
So that his own herd boys drove him off,
And his dogs bite his thighs.

Inanna, or Ishtar, is associated with Tammuz, the dying and rising god of vegetation, whom she seeks in the underworld in his season of recession, according to the motif of the search of the fertility-goddess for the dying and rising god of vegetation. This motif recurs in Canaan in the search of the goddess Anat for the dead Baal, in Egypt in the search of Isis for Horus, in Greece in Demeter's search for Kore ('the Maiden') and Aphrodite's for Adonis. The activity of Ishtar in the period of the eclipse of the fertility-god may reflect her significance in irrigation in the dry season. This is suggested by the role of the god Athtar in the Ras Shamra texts from Canaan, where he proves an inadequate substitute for the dead Baal, the god of winter rain, and, obliged to evacuate Baal's throne, descends to be 'lord of the underworld, all of it'. Indeed, Ishtar and Athtar may well be etymologically connected with the Arabic verb *'athara* meaning 'to irrigate'.

Ishtar, however, is known in the Semitic period in Babylon and in Assyria as a warrior-goddess, and this is her role in her Canaanite development as Anat. This attribute is probably specifically a Semitic development and may be associated with the character of the Semitic god Athtar. He is manifest in the Venus star, the most significant star in the Near East, called by the Arabs in Palestine *an-najm*, 'the star'. This god was venerated as an astral god in southern Arabia, second only to the moon-god and the sun-goddess. He was also venerated among the Arabs in the caravan city of Palmyra in the first three centuries A.D., and among the neighbours of Israel in Moab and Ammon. There the god was entitled 'the King', *malik-ma*, which was parodied by orthodox Jewish scribes in the Old Testament as *Milcom*, using the vowels of the Hebrew word for 'abomination'. The association of Ishtar-Athtar with war may derive from the significance of the bright

Seal-impression from Tell Asmar representing the sacred marriage of the god and the goddess of fertility, represented by the king and a priestess (mid-third millennium B.C.). Iraq Museum.

Stele of an Assyrian governor (eighth century B.C.) standing before Adad, characterised by his lightning-bolts, and his associate the fertility-goddess, the warlike Ishtar of Arbela, from Babylon. Istanbul Archaeological Museum.

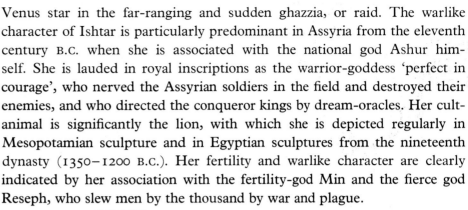

Venus star in the far-ranging and sudden ghazzia, or raid. The warlike character of Ishtar is particularly predominant in Assyria from the eleventh century B.C. when she is associated with the national god Ashur himself. She is lauded in royal inscriptions as the warrior-goddess 'perfect in courage', who nerved the Assyrian soldiers in the field and destroyed their enemies, and who directed the conqueror kings by dream-oracles. Her cult-animal is significantly the lion, with which she is depicted regularly in Mesopotamian sculpture and in Egyptian sculptures from the nineteenth dynasty (1350–1200 B.C.). Her fertility and warlike character are clearly indicated by her association with the fertility-god Min and the fierce god Reseph, who slew men by the thousand by war and plague.

NEBO AND MARDUK

In the Assyrian sculpture on this page, certain emblems appear along with the deities Ashur and Ishtar, namely a spear-head, a wedge, or perhaps a stylus, with a crescent moon. The crescent symbolises the moon-god Sin. The wedge was the symbol of Nebo, the divine patron of writing and speech, the Mercury of the Babylonian pantheon. The name Nebo, the speaker for the gods, who had the means of expression available to men, is possibly associated with the Hebrew word for 'prophet' *(nabhi')*.

In this sculpture the spear-head was the symbol of Marduk. He had been the city-god of Babylon in the Amorite period (1826–1526 B.C.) and assimilated the role of the Sumerian Enlil as the executive of the divine court and as the storm-god. As such, he plays the protagonist's role in the conflict of Order with primeval Chaos culminating in creation, which belonged to the liturgy of the festival at the spring New Year, the chief seasonal crisis in Mesopotamia. Those functions were assumed also by Adad among the Amorites of northern Mesopotamia. He was called Hadad in Syria and Palestine, where his predominant role was recognised by his title Baal ('the lord'). His role in the conflict with the powers of Chaos in the liturgy of the New Year festival in Assyria was assumed by Ashur, the national god of Assyria, who is shown armed with lightning in combat with the monster of Chaos in a sculpture from the palace of Ashurnasirpal II (883–859 B.C.) at Nimrud, ancient Kalhu.

ERESHKIGAL AND NERGAL

Two other deities from the vast pantheon of ancient Mesopotamia deserve special mention. These are the sinister powers of the underworld, Ereshkigal and Nergal.

Two myths, which give the fullest picture of the ancient Mesopotamian idea of the underworld, indicate a development in the conception of the supreme deity of the underworld. According to the well known text related to the fertility-cult, in which the fertility-goddess Ishtar descends to the underworld through seven gates, at each of which she is gradually divested of all that symbolises her divine authority, the queen of those infernal regions is the goddess Ereshkigal, or Allatu ('the goddess'). Another myth describes how Nergal, the god of mass destruction by war or plague, penetrated the underworld, posting his own guards at each of its fourteen gates. He dethroned Ereshkigal, but spared her life when she entreated him to marry her and take over her realm. The weapons of Nergal, heat, lightning and plague, indicate his function as a solar deity.

Left: brick-moulding of the fertility-goddess Ishtar as dispenser of never-failing water, from the facade of a Kassite temple at Uruk (fifteenth century B.C.).

Below: relief on an alabaster vase from the temple of Inanna, the fertility-goddess, characterised by the looped reed-bundles, to whom a priest, possibly the king, offers fruits (c. 3500-3250 B.C.). Iraq Museum.

The Myths

The myths which the Semites of Mesopotamia inherited from the Sumerians and developed present a colourful if somewhat bewildering kaleidoscope. They are all highly entertaining, particularly the epic of the adventures of Gilgamesh, the ancient king of Uruk. This story, whatever its original significance, was probably enjoyed in convivial gatherings, like the Arabian Nights and other tales in Arab coffee halls nearer our own time. This popularity is suggested by the fragment of a clay tablet of the epic found as far afield as Megiddo in Palestine from about the twelfth century B.C. Generally, however, the myths show signs of a different origin. In spite of the dramatic character they share with the Gilgamesh Legend, their protagonists are not men but gods, usually deified forces of nature, portrayed with stark anthropomorphism. Yet they reveal the thought of the philosophers of the day, the priests who employed their learned leisure in the great temple estates to understand the origin of their world and to adjust man to his environment.

Thus some myths deal with origins. Others deal with relationships in nature and society, recognising, if not solving, the problem of contradictory forces in an economy which in other ways showed so much evidence of the harmony and order that the Sumerian, and later the Semitic, mind strove to discover. In such myths, however crude they may seem to Western ears, this assumption of an explicable order in spite of tension may be discerned. The same mind was at work here as in the classified lists of natural forces and substances, such as plants, precious stones and other objects, which the ancient Mesopotamians adduced as evidence of their recognition of this order, and which is reflected by the determinative signs which introduce nouns in the cuneiform script according to their categories. If, despite this relative sophistication, we find a dramatic naivete and even crudity, this is not remarkable, but simply betokens the intense involvement which the ancient Mesopotamian felt with the world about him; it is a survival of primitive animism. Where there were such rich natural agricultural resources to exploit, man could not fail to be conscious of his own potential. Yet he was always conscious of his limitations because of the hazards of his physical environment. Mesopotamia lay between the two capricious river giants, Tigris and Euphrates, which could lay a district waste for a generation in one spring flood. It bordered the desert with its dust-storms, blasting simooms, locust swarms and raiding Bedouin. Thus the drama and the anthropomorphism of Mesopotamian mythology express the essentially emotional relationship of man to his environment in what we, though not he, would regard as both its natural and supernatural aspect.

This emotional involvment is particularly apparent in myth in relation to ritual. Thus in the great festival at the spring equinox, when order was menaced by the spring floods, man co-operated with the deified forces of nature in the conflict between Order and Chaos. He expressed his anxieties and his hopes, at once relieving his great emotional tension at the great seasonal crisis, influencing the powers of Providence by auto-suggestion and renewing his faith that his god, his help in ages past, was his hope for years to come. This significance of myth, used in its precise Greek sense of *muthos*, the 'word' which accompanies ritual to make its meaning explicit to the worshippers and, by articulate expression, to make it doubly effective, is a most important element in ancient religion.

THE BABYLONIAN NEW YEAR FESTIVAL

This means of engaging the worshippers actively and intelligently and of influencing Providence by auto-suggestion is particularly well exemplified in the myth from the liturgy of the spring New Year festival at Babylon. The sacramental celebration of the critical conflict of Cosmos and Chaos, resulting in the triumph of the divine champion of Order, had its local counterparts, as we shall see, in the nature-religion of Canaan and indeed in Israel itself, where it was the source of the great conception of the Kingship of God. This great theme developed beyond the sphere of nature and, projected in Israel to the plane of history and morality, is one of the major themes of the theology of Israel. It gives coherence to much of the Old Testament thought, and indeed to the thought of the whole Bible. It will be found to give coherence also to the present study on the mythology of the Semites in Mesopotamia, Canaan and Israel.

The Babylonian version of this theme, known as *enuma elish* ('When on high') from the opening words of the myth, accompanied the ritual of the Babylonian New Year festival on the fourth of the eleven days of the celebrations. The text was recovered from copies in Ashurbanipal's library at Nineveh and from fragments from southern Mesopotamia. The earliest extant fragment is from the first millennium B.C., but on grounds of language and style the myth may confidently be carried back to an original, early in the second millennium B.C., and it was in use when the Amorite Hammurabi ruled Babylon in about 1700.

Right: bronze amulet figurine of the Mesopotamian demon Pazuzu, with the feet and claws of an eagle, and a monster head, partly of a lion. Louvre.

Below: lion-headed eagle spreading its wings over two stags from above the doorway of a temple at al-Ubaid near Ur. In hammered copper, early second millennium B.C. British Museum.

This festival was a real occasion of renewal. As usual at such crises, normal activity was suspended, and the first four days were reckoned outside the calendar. According to a refrain to the myth, this was in sympathy with the temporary confinement of the god Marduk 'in the mountain'; that is to say, in the underworld. On the fifth day the temple was sprinkled with water and fumigated with incense. In a rite resembling that of the scapegoat in Israel, the disabilities of the community were concentrated in a sheep, which was then beheaded. The body was rubbed on the walls of the shrine of Nebo, the divine advocate and mediator between gods and men. The severed head and body were then thrown into the river to be swept away from the settlement, as the scapegoat in Israel was taken out into the desert to be thrown over a cliff to its death. This rite, so reminiscent of the Jewish atonement ritual (Hebrew *kippur*), was in fact called 'atonement' (Akkadian *kupparu*). Those who officiated at the rite were sent out of the city into a desert place, where they remained till the end of the festival.

On the same day the king, the focus of the vitality of the community and its contact with the gods, ceremonially abdicated his office in the temple of Marduk. As the culmination of the ceremony, he was divested of his regalia and buffeted and abused by the priest, after which he knelt humbly before the image of the god Marduk and disavowed all tyranny and injustice and abuse of his office. This was the turning-point of the drama. In anticipation of the emergence of the god from his confinement and his victory over the forces of Chaos, the king was reinvested with his symbols of rule, and grasped the hands of the image of Marduk to symbolise his reinstatement as vice-regent of the god. The ritual was completed by a curious rite. The priest sharply slapped the king's face again. If this forced tears it was taken as a good omen. It has been thought that this was the survival of a rite of imitative magic to induce rain, but it may have been designed to emphasise further the king's dependence on the god, just as 'servant', really 'slave', of God was a royal title in ancient Canaan and in Judah. It may also have been the test of how sincerely and seriously the king accepted his office and those aspects of it which the rites symbolised.

On the sixth day the theme of the ritual was the arrival of Nebo, regarded as the son of Marduk, from neighbouring Borsippa, his cult-centre. The theme of the seventh day's ritual was Nebo's liberation of Marduk.

The ritual continued on the eighth day with the celebration of Marduk's investiture with the kingship by the council of the gods, and with a triumphal procession and celebration of Marduk's victory on the ninth day. On the

Amorite seal-impression (*c.* 1830-1350 B.C.) depicting a warrior, or king, introduced by a minor god to Ishtar characterised by her lion. Pierpont Morgan Library, New York.

tenth day there was feasting, celebrating the banquet of the gods as a 'rite of integration' after the passing of the crisis. The union of the god and the fertility-goddess was also celebrated on this occasion.

Up to this point the vicissitudes of the god Marduk seem to be those characteristic of the dying and rising god of vegetation, with a counterpart in the myth of Baal's conflict with Death or Sterility *(mot)* in the Canaanite texts from the Ras Shamra (see page 88). It is possible that a local rite from an autumn festival in the cult of the vegetation god, called in Mesopotamia Tammuz, has been fused with the conception of Marduk's triumph over the cosmic forces of disorder which is the basis of the myth *enuma elîsh*. Marduk's victory has its Canaanite counterpart in Baal's conflict with, and victory over, the unruly waters (see page 79).

The Babylonian festival ended in 'the fixing of destinies' in nature and society for the coming year, which was the theme of the eleventh day. On the twelfth day the images of the gods were returned to their various temples.

THE BABYLONIAN CREATION MYTH

In this context of ritual renewal of nature and society, the myth *enuma elîsh*, often called 'the Babylonian Creation Myth', was recited on the fourth day.

The first three of its seven large tablets describe the creation of the Mesopotamian pantheon:

When on high the heaven had not been named,
Firm ground below had not been called by name,
There was nought but primordial Apsu, their begetter,
And Mother Tiamat, who bore them all,
Their waters commingling in a single body;
No reed hut had been matted, no marsh land had appeared,
When no gods whatever had been brought into being,
Uncalled by name, their destinies undetermined,
Then it was that the gods were formed within them,
Lahmu and Lahamu were brought forth, by name they were called,
Before they were grown in age and stature,
Anshar and Kishar were formed, surpassing the others,
They prolonged the days, accumulated the years,
Anu was their heir, of his fathers the rival,
Yea, Anshar's firstborn, Anu, was his equal,
Anu begot in his image Nudimmud,

. . . . . .

In this introduction to the myth we have the effort of Mesopotamian sages to explain first origins.

The inert forces of Apsu and Tiamat and the primordial gods resent the purposeful activity of the younger, effective gods of the Mesopotamian

The fertility-goddess Ishtar,
dispenser of 'living water' from a
never-failing jar, in a sculpture
from Mari of the Amorite period
(c. nineteenth century B.C.)
National Museum, Aleppo.

Assyrian relief of the storm-god
Adad, Sumerian Enlil,
brandishing lightning-bolts, on
his cult-animal the bull. Louvre.

pantheon, Anu, the sky-god and the divine king paramount, Enki, also called Ea and Nudimmud, the god of controlled water, and others. Apprehending repression by the primordial powers, Ea, who is also the god of wisdom, cunning and spells as well as of water, overcomes Apsu by his art and imposes his control over him, reflecting control over the sweet waters as the first stage in the civilisation of southern Mesopotamia. Then Marduk is born to Ea. The description of Marduk, the city-god of Babylon in the Amorite period, hence a comparative upstart, indicates that in the Sumerian original the god was Enlil, the god of the storm-wind, who was to become the executive of the royal power of Anu.

The resentment of the forces of primordial Chaos mounts, and their menace under the championship of Tiamat is great enough to dismay Anu and his celestial court. Anshar, the father of Anu, and the celestials find none to respond to the challenge of Tiamat. For the ancient Mesopotamian, as for all serious men, faith might assert the beneficence and power of God, but experience was painfully aware of the reality of suffering and uncertainty in nature and society. Tiamat prepares for open war, and a monstrous brood is spawned for this purpose by a primordial mother-goddess Hubur. Among these a commander-in-chief, Kingu, is appointed and invested with the Tablets of Destiny, the divine blue-print, like the 'word of God' in Israel, which it is his commission to carry into effect.

The second part of the myth describes how Marduk is singled out as the champion of the divine court, undertakes the commission and is invested with the kingship to sustain the royal authority of Anu and the heavenly court against the menace of primeval Chaos. At this point there is a feature curiously reminiscent of the sign of Gideon's fleece and the dew (Judges 6.36–40) and of the signs of the leprous hand and the rod and the serpent, which authenticate Moses' mission (Exodus 4.1–7). It consists of a sign through a piece of cloth on the ground, which will vanish and reappear, an indication of a common stock-in-trade of saga themes in the ancient Near East, of which other instances could be cited. After the preliminary taunts and insulting challenges characteristic of Semitic war poetry, Marduk engages Tiamat in single combat, armed with bow, mace, lightning, net and winds. The storm-god rides in his chariot drawn by a team of four, the Killer, the Relentless, the Trampler and the Swift, an indication of the original role of Enlil in the myth. Symbolic armament of a similar kind will also be seen as a feature of the Canaanite myth of Baal and the unruly waters, and it is significant that one of Baal's stock epithets in those texts is 'He who mounts the clouds'. This is also a title of the God of Israel in the vindication of his kingship against the menace of disorder (Psalms 68.4 and elsewhere). At the height of the conflict:

The Evil Wind, which followed behind, he let loose in her face.
When Tiamat opened her mouth to consume him,
He drove in the Evil Wind that she closed not her lips.
As the fierce winds charged her belly,
Her body was distended and her mouth was wide open.
He released the arrow, it tore her belly,
It cut through her insides, splitting the heart.
Having thus subdued her, he extinguished her life.
He cast down her carcase to stand upon it.

The allies of Tiamat are slain or captured and imprisoned and the Tablets of Destiny are taken from Kingu and fixed by Marduk on his own breast, so that control of the world should be under the proper authority of the heavenly court.

As the first token of his efficient power to uphold Order against the menace of Chaos, Marduk proceeds to complete creation:

The lord trod on the legs of Tiamat,
With his unsparing mace he crushed her skull.
When the arteries of her blood he had severed,
He split her like a shell-fish into two parts;
Half of her he set up and ceiled it as sky,
Pulled down the bar and posted guards.
He bade them to allow not her waters to escape.
He quartered the heavens and surveyed the regions.
He squared Apsu's quarter, the abode of Nudimmud,
As the lord measured the dimensions of Apsu.
The Great Abode, its likeness, he fixed as Esharra,
The Great Abode, Esharra, which he made as the firmament,
Anu, Enlil and Ea he made occupy their places.

He constructed stations for the great gods,
Fixing their astral likenesses as constellations.
He determined the year by designating the zones:
He set up three constellations for each of the twelve months.
After defining the days of the year by means of heavenly figures,
He founded the station of Nebiru to determine their heavenly bands,
That none might transgress or fall short.
. . . . .

The Moon he caused to shine, the night to him entrusting,
He appointed him a creature of the night to signify the days.

Finally the great gods with Marduk create man out of the blood of Kingu, the commander-in-chief of Tiamat's horde, a recognition perhaps of the daemonic, rebellious element in human nature. There is an interesting variant of this tradition in a Babylonian and an Assyrian version. In this version primitive man, *lullu*, the Mesopotamian counterpart of Adam in Genesis, is created by the mother-goddess Ninhursag, the primordial earth-mound, out of clay. The blood of a slain god was used to animate the man in accordance with the ancient belief, found also in the Old Testament (Deuteronomy 12.23), that the blood was the life-essence.

In the myth *enuma elish* it is emphasised that man was created for the service of the great gods, to manage their estates and liberate them from drudgery.

In honour of Marduk's victory his temple is built on its massive staged tower *(ziggurat)*, 'the Tower of Babel' of early Hebrew legend (Genesis 11.1–9). This was the work of the great gods, the last of their labours. The building of the temple of the god, which was also his palace and in Mesopotamia the manor-house of his estate, sets the seal on the establishment of his royal authority. This motif recurs in Canaanite mythology in the myth of Baal's struggle with the forces of Chaos (see page 81) and in its Hebrew development, and is most notably expressed in Micah 4.1–3 and Isaiah 2.2 ff.:

And it shall come to pass in the latter days,
That the mountain of the house of the Lord
Shall be established as the highest of the mountains . . .

There follows a 'house-warming', which is also a feature of the completion of the 'house of Baal' in Canaanite mythology (see page 82) and may be the prototype of the Lord's grim feast on His 'day', when He shall make His royal authority effective to the discomfiture of all who oppose Him (Zephaniah 1.7 ff). This reflects a rite of integration when all relaxed after the tension of crisis, and the 'merriment' of the gods was a sign for similar 'merriment' among the worshippers. We may picture the scene from the description of a feast of the gods at another point in the myth:

They kissed one another in the assembly,
They held converse as they sat down to the banquet.
They ate festive bread, poured the wine,
They wetted their drinking-tubes with sweet intoxicant,
As they drank the strong drink their bodies swelled,
They became very languid as their spirits arose.

Then the triumphant god, significantly named Enlil, a survival of the original Sumerian version, proudly displays his weapons, which were made into constellations, including the bow-star. The text ends with a hymn of praise to Marduk-Enlil by the gods. He is acclaimed by fifty names or honorific titles, each one of which is declared to be symbolic of some attribute, exploit or activity of the god. Such titles, in the form of participles, are a feature of Hebrew Hymns of Praise to God, many of which have their proper place in the acclamation of his nature and exploits in his victorious conflict with the powers of chaos and his advent as king in the context of the New Year festival.

ISHTAR'S DESCENT TO THE UNDERWORLD

In the nature religion of the Near East the vicissitudes of the deities associated with vegetation reflect the seasonal flourishing and wilting of growth in those regions, which is so sharply contrasting as to suggest life and death. The motif of the death of the fertility-god and his detention in the underworld is familiar. Thus Kore, the Maiden, daughter of Demeter the earth-mother in Greek mythology, was carried off to the infernal realm of Dis. In the Canaanite Baal myth, which reflects seasonal ritual, we shall see Baal overcome by Mot (Death, Sterility) in the underworld, whence his body is recovered for burial by the goddesses Shapash ('the sun') and Anat, the chief fertility-goddess, his sister. In Mesopotamia Dumuzi, or Tammuz, was regarded as annually

Seal-impression, possibly north Syrian, of the nude fertility-goddess enclosed in what may be a rainbow and associated with a bull, the cult-animal of her associate, the fertility-god Adad. The worshipper on the left bears a hawk and the one on the right, apparently female, wears a head-dress with apparently the hooded cobra of Egyptian royalty. The object before the latter may be a native rendering of the Egyptian *djed*, or symbol of the renewal and permanence of the dynasty. There is a strange mixture of motifs, rather suggestive of Mitannian seals.

descending to the underworld, and one of the most familiar themes of Mesopotamian mythology, doubtless related to a seasonal ritual at the height of the hot season, is the descent of the fertility-goddess Sumerian Inanna, Semitic Ishtar, to the underworld. The story is contained in the Akkadian version from the end of the second millennium B.C. from Ashur, the old religious capital of Assyria.

The text opens with a description of the underworld, as gloomy and insubstantial as the prospect of the after-life in Israel until the emergence of a livelier hope just before the Christian era:

To the Land of No Return, the realm of Ereshkigal,
Ishtar the daughter of Sin set her mind.
Yea, the daughter of Sin set her mind
To the dark house, the abode of Irkalla,
To the house which none leave who have entered it,
To the road from which there is no way back,
To the house wherein the entrants are bereft of life,
Where dust is their fare and clay their food,
Where they see no light, residing in darkness,
Where they are clothed like birds, with wings for garments,
And where over door and bolt is spread dust.

Arriving at the gate of the underworld, the lusty goddess, who was as potent in war as in love in Mesopotamian religion, threatens to burst in by force. She is admitted by order of Ereshkigal, the queen of the underworld, on condition that she leaves part of her clothing and insignia at each of the seven gates she is to pass. Then with verbal repetition characteristic of ritual texts and of epic style, a strip-tease act ensues, after which the goddess stands naked within the seventh gate. In the presence of Ereshkigal she flies at the queen of the underworld. But, like Samson shorn of his hair, she discovers too late that she is now powerless. She is seized and confined and afflicted with various disabilities by order of Ereshkigal, with dire repercussions in the land of the living:

The bull springs not upon the cow, the ass impregnates not the jenny,
In the street the man impregnates not the maiden.

Meanwhile the god of water, and of wisdom and magic, Ea, undertakes to revive and restore Ishtar to the land of the living so that normal fertility may be restored. He creates a eunuch, whom he sends to Ereshkigal. The natural instinct of the queen of the underworld is thus aroused, and on the instruction of Ea the eunuch presumes on her fondness to ask for a drink from the water-skin containing life-giving water. This would be tantamount to seeking dismissal from the underworld, and so she curses him. Ea evidently contrived this, so that her curse should be exhausted and its potency against Ishtar consequently impaired, just as Isaac exhausted his blessing to Jacob, so that Esau could no longer benefit as he should (Genesis 27.33 ff). So Ereshkigal, evidently to prevent any further stratagems from Ea and the high gods, gives orders to 'sprinkle Ishtar with the water of life and take her from my presence'. The goddess returns through the seven gates, at each of which her insignia and her clothes are restored.

The text closes with a mention of a ransom which must be paid by Ishtar so that she may not return to the dead. This probably related to a sacrifice. Here too, rather abruptly, the revival of her lover, the fertility-god Tammuz, is visualised:

Combat of the god, probably
Ashur, as sustainer of Cosmos
against the monster of Chaos, the
Assyrian version of the theme of
the Babylonian New Year liturgy,
from the palace of Ashurnasirpal II
(883-859 B.C.) at Nimrud,
ancient Kalhu. British Museum.

As for Tammuz, the lover of her youth,
Wash him with pure water, anoint him with sweet oil;
Clothe him with a red garment, let him play on a flute of lapis lazuli.
Let courtesans turn his mood.

The text ends with an invocation:
May the dead rise and smell the incense.

This probably alludes to the conception that the dead in the underworld
have an influence on the fertility of the soil. Similarly Hesiod ascribes a
fertility function to the dead of the golden and silver ages. Also he tells how
the daughters of Danaos poured water into bottomless jars as a fertility rite
to enlist the favour of the dead. The Mesopotamian text was once probably
part of a seasonal fertility rite, and the final invocation may have been used to
provoke the potency of the dead in fertility.

It is important to understand the relevance to daily life of the great myths
which asserted man's faith that the great gods in their prevailing sovereignty
and beneficence would bring Order out of primeval Chaos and would maintain it against the recurring menace of Chaos in the great seasonal crisis.
The recalling of the creative and ordering activity of the great gods was a
means of renewing this faith in the emergencies of daily life. Thus, the

36

account of the creation of man by the mother-goddess, who compounded him of clay and the blood of a slain god, was used as an incantation. It was accompanied by the moulding of wombs and sexual organs in clay and the simulation of a birth as a rite of imitative magic, as is evident from the passage at the end of the extant text:

As the Bearing One gives birth,
May the mother of the child bring forth by herself.

Even such a minor affliction as the toothache was treated with such an incantation, which recounted the origin of the malady in the divine economy and in so doing sought to control it. An incantation of this type is known from the Amorite texts from Mari on the mid-Euphrates in the first half of the second millennium B.C. Another may be cited from the neo-Babylonian period (late seventh to late sixth century B.C.):

After Anu had created heaven,
Heaven had created earth,
The earth had created the rivers,
The rivers had created the canals,
The canals had created the marsh,
And the marsh had created the worm –
The worm went weeping before Shamash,
His tears flowing before Ea:

'What wilt thou give me for my food?
What wilt thou give me for my sucking?'
'I shall give thee the ripe fig,
And the apricot.'
'Of what use are they to me, the ripe fig,
And the apricot?
Lift me up among the teeth,
And among the gums cause me to dwell.
The blood of the tooth I will suck,
And of the gum I will gnaw its roots.'

The text ends with prescriptions for extraction and for the threefold repetition of the text as an incantation.

In all their keen observation and awareness of the harmony and tension in nature and society, it would have been surprising if the ancient Mesopotamians had not been arrested by the paradox of man, 'the glory, jest and riddle of the world'. We have seen their recognition of man's affinity with God in the conception of his creation from the blood of a god, albeit a rebellious one. Man is nevertheless created to serve the gods, to do their drudgery or to manage their estates, as the *ensi*, or tenant-farmer, of the god. The natural limitation of such a person, who was yet the repository of so much authority, wisdom and skill, posed a problem for thinking men. This problem is the subject of two notable texts, which have as their heroes Adapa, an ancient chief-priest of Eridu, the cult-centre of Ea, and the ancient priest-king Gilgamesh of Uruk (Biblical Erech), who was 'two-thirds as a god and one-third human'.

THE MYTH OF ADAPA

The myth of Adapa is known from a fragment on a clay tablet which was used as a school text for scribes in the chancellery of the Egyptian capital at Tell el-Amarna in the fourteenth century B.C. It is also known from three other fragments from the great royal library of Ashurbanipal (664–626 B.C.) at Nineveh.

Adapa is introduced to us as the sage priest of Ea, who had imparted his own wisdom to him:

His command was like the command of Ea,
Wise understanding he had perfected for him to disclose the designs of the land.
To him he had given wisdom; eternal life he had not given him.
In those days, in those years, the sage from Eridu,
Ea, created him as the model of men.
The sage—his command no man can vitiate—
The capable, the most wise among the Anunnaki is he;
The blameless, the clean of hands, the anointment priest, the observer of rites.
With the bakers he does the baking,
With the bakers of Eridu he does the baking,
Bread and water for Eridu he daily provides,
With his clean hands he arranges the offering table,
Without him the table cannot be cleared.
He steers the ship, he does the prescribed fishing for Eridu.

Out fishing one day in a lagoon of the lower Euphrates, Adapa, when his boat is upset by a squall from the south, curses the south wind. His curse is effective: 'the wing of the south wind was broken'.

Thereupon Anu, the celestial King paramount, incensed and even alarmed that a mortal should be so far versed in wisdom and in the control of nature, summons Adapa before the celestial court. His patron Ea instructs him to obey and appear in the guise of a mourner and a penitent. He will be met at the gate of heaven by the minor gods Tammuz and Gizidu, who will speak kindly to Adapa and introduce him to Anu, in whose presence he will be offered bread and water and oil for refreshment. Ea advises Adapa not to accept this, because it is the bread and the water of death. Adapa is questioned and admits that he had laid a potent curse on the south wind. The significant question is then asked:

Why did Ea to a worthless human of the heaven
And of the earth the plan disclose,
Rendering him distinguished and making a name for him?

This is strongly reminiscent of the divine resentment at Adam for presuming to eat of the tree of knowledge of good and evil.

The question is then posed what should be done about the situation. The exclusive prerogative of the gods might be safeguarded by destroying Adapa, which would have seemed by the best of human standards unworthy

Mitannian seal-impression from Mesopotamia depicting a goddess facing a god, who drinks beer out of a tube. British Museum.

of the gods. Another solution would be to promote Adapa to the ranks of the immortals by offering him what actually was the bread and water of life, and that is what is done. But, mindful of Ea's warning, Adapa refuses, and so forfeits immortality. The subtlety which his patron Ea had inculcated into him is shown to fall short of the wisdom and insight of the gods. Adapa is but man and remains mortal; and so, ridiculed at the last by Anu, Adapa is dismissed unceremoniously to earth and mortality. Perhaps Ea had already rued the measure of divine wisdom he had imparted to Adapa and had deliberately misled him with his warning; perhaps Anu played a cruel jest on Adapa. In any case it is obvious that it is not the will of the gods that man, for all his potential, should be immortal as the gods, and to this end the gods exploit man's own wisdom, which in the last instance is limited by its experiential caution. This obstructs his faith and makes him painfully conscious of his own deficiency.

THE GILGAMESH EPIC

The famous Gilgamesh Epic, or Legend, survives in twelve tablets in Akkadian from the middle of the second millennium B.C., with fragments from Palestine from about 1200 B.C. and from the Hittite capital Boghazköi in Asia Minor. The Legend is the final elaboration of a saga cycle of incidents associated with Gilgamesh, the king of the Sumerian city of Uruk in the first quarter of the third millennium B.C. That he really lived is indicated in a Sumerian fragment in epic style from the first half of the second millennium B.C., which records a war between Gilgamesh and the king of Kish. Gilgamesh was beseiged in his city by the king and was grateful to accept his rival's terms. Thus, like King Arthur, he is a historical figure, though better known in legend than history.

The opening of the text, 'He who saw everything' *(sa nagbe imuru)*, by which it is known in Mesopotamian literature, is curiously suggestive of the opening of Homer's *Odyssey*, with which it is not unworthy to be compared in scope and profundity. Indeed it may be said to be more profound, since its highly entertaining narrative episodes are more strictly subordinate to the philosophic theme of the contrast between man's gifts and high aspirations and his physical limitations. The predominance of this philosophic theme puts the text, for all its epic form, into the category of books of wisdom, and it may well have been this influence which first created a literary unity out of the saga tradition of Gilgamesh.

As in Greek tragedy, man is represented by a figure of heroic proportions, in whom the problems of human destiny may be brought into sharp focus on a spectacular stage. In the king man finds his closest affinity to the gods in the ancient Semitic world, as is expressed in the Akkadian saying:

Man, being the king,
Who is as the image of God.

Thus the problems of mankind are reflected in the experience of King Gilgamesh, who is 'two-thirds a god and one-third human', which incidentally may be reflected in the legend of a race, 'the mighty men of renown', who were born of the union of human women with the 'sons of God' in Genesis 6.1–4.

The Gilgamesh Legend opens somewhat surprisingly with the thrice-repeated complaint of the nobles of Uruk that:

Gilgamesh leaves not the son to his father;
Day and night unbridled is his arrogance;
. . . . . .
Gilgamesh leaves not the maid to her mother,
The warrior's daughter, the noble's spouse.

This may be an incidental criticism of absolutism, including the *ius primae noctis*, the right of a lord to take the virginity of the daughters of his vassals. Or it may be a reflection on the selfish impulse of human nature unbridled by limitations. Or it may simply emphasise the freedom of a king from the normal limitations of ordinary men, just as the sage in Ecclesiastes casts himself hypothetically in the role of 'king in Jerusalem' with all that man could normally seek for his satisfaction and fulfilment, in order to emphasise the essential limitations of human life (Ecclesiastes 1.12–2.26).

GILGAMESH AND ENKIDU

In the context of the Gilgamesh Legend the passage serves to introduce Enkidu, the wild man of the steppe, first an antagonist worthy of the mettle of Gilgamesh and then his faithful companion in his heroic exploits. The creation of Enkidu is an interesting variation of the Mesopotamian conception of man fashioned out of the clay of the earth, with the addition of his being conceived in the image of the high god and celestial ruler. A certain goddess Aru conceived the idea of a double of Anu, and, washing her hands, 'pinched off clay' and cast it in the divine image on the steppe. In both particulars, the substance of man and the image of God, this is the conception of the creation of man in Genesis 2.7. Indeed, in the late wisdom of the Book of Job, the same imagery and the same verb are used in the statement of the sage Elihu (Job 33.6):

I stand in the same relationship to God as yourself,
I too was nipped off from the clay.

Enkidu is depicted as a wild man, who 'knows neither people nor land', but 'feeds on grass with the gazelles' and 'jostles with the wild beasts at the waterhole', an association which was broken after Enkidu's contact with civilisation. The relationship of Enkidu with the beasts as well as with Gilgamesh, the symbol of sophisticated urban civilisation, reflects the interest of Mesopotamian sages in the harmony and tension in nature and society, man and brutes, the solitary and the political man, the town-dweller and the Bedouin of the steppe, the potential enemy or ally of the town-dweller in Mesopotamia. The taming of Enkidu is the first of the exploits of Gilgamesh, which may reflect the adjustment of relations with the Bedouin that was regarded as the first task of the rulers of the Mesopotamian city-states. Before Gilgamesh and Enkidu could come to grips, however, the ground is prepared by the cunning of a hunter, who is persuaded to humanise the wild man by contriving that he mate with a woman. A temple prostitute is sent by Gilgamesh. She waits for Enkidu by the waterhole, and the mating takes place 'for six days and seven nights', then

After he had had (his) fill of her charms,
He set his face towards the wild beasts.

But the metamorphosis has been effected:

'. . . man's dominion
had broken nature's social union'.

On seeing him, the gazelles run off,

The wild beasts of the steppe drew away from his body;
Startled was Enkidu, his body became taut,
His knees were motionless—for his wild beasts had gone.
Enkidu had to slacken his pace—it was not as before;
But he now had wisdom, broader understanding.

He returns to the harlot, who proposes to introduce him to his new society in the city of Uruk, persuading him with the prospect of animal satisfaction, the joyous abandon of festivals, lusty lasses and Gilgamesh, who

Like a wild ox lords it over the folk.
The strength of Gilgamesh is an irresistible challenge.

Gilgamesh is warned of the coming of Enkidu, an epoch-making event in his life, by two dreams: one of a star which fell from the sky and proved an immovable obstruction, and the other of an axe which lay in his path.

The two eventually meet and a quarrel is provoked by Enkidu, resulting in an epic wrestling match:

They met in the Market-of-the-Land,
Enkidu barred the gate
With his foot,
Not allowing Gilgamesh to enter.
They grappled each other,
Holding fast like bulls.
They shattered the doorpost,
As the wall shook.
Gilgamesh and Enkidu
Grappled each other,
Holding fast like bulls;
They shattered the doorpost,
As the wall shook.
As Gilgamesh crooked the knee,
His foot on the ground—
His fury abated
And he turned away.
When he had turned away,
Enkidu to him
Speaks up, to Gilgamesh:
'As one alone thy mother
Bore thee,
The wild cow of the steer-folds,
Ninsunna.
Raised up above man is thy head,
Kingship over the people
Enlil has granted thee!'

THE EXPLOIT AGAINST THE GIANT HUWAWA

The two then embark on a series of notable exploits. These exemplify the theme that, if man must accept his mortality and inferiority to the gods, he may yet win a name for himself and so live in posterity:

Who, my friend, can scale the heavens?
Only the gods live forever under the sun.
As for mankind, numbered are their days;
Whatever they achieve is but wind!
Even here thou art afraid of death.
What of thy heroic might?
Let me go before thee,
Let thy mouth call to me, "Advance, fear not!"
Should I fall, I shall have made me a name:
'Gilgamesh'—they will say—'against fierce Huwawa
Has fallen!' (Long) after
My offspring has been born in my house.

Akkadian seal-impression (late third millennium B.C.) depicting an exploit of Gilgamesh and Enkidu. Royal Dutch Cabinet of Medals, The Hague.

So replies Gilgamesh to Enkidu, whose realism at this point serves as a foil to the bold enterprise of Gilgamesh in their first exploit to subdue Huwawa, also called Humbaba, the giant guardian of the cedar forest. This probably reflects the historical tradition of long expeditions from Mesopotamia, which has no heavy timber, to Syria, probably rather to the Amanus range in northern Syria than to the Lebanon. If the description of 'the cedar mountain' as 'the abode of the gods' is literal, as it may well be, this might indicate specifically Mt. Saphon, twenty miles north of Ras Shamra, which was the seat of Baal in the Ras Shamra myths. Professor Shaeffer discovered an ancient cult-place there. The description of the encounter with Huwawa, however, indicates a volcano:

Huwawa—his roaring is the flood-storm,
His mouth is fire,
His breath is death!

This, if it indeed denotes a volcano, cannot refer to the Amanus or Lebanon, but since it is reported by Enkidu from the days when he roamed the steppe, it might denote the volcanoes of the Jebel Druze known to the Mesopotamians from the reports of Bedouin caravaneers.

Despite the discouragement from the elders of Uruk and inauspicious omens from Shamash, the sun-god, who was the patron of Gilgamesh, the pair set out on their journey, which, in heroic convention, is accomplished at the rate of fifty leagues each day:

At twenty leagues they broke off for a morsel,
At thirty leagues they prepared for the night.

They arrive at the entrance to the cedar forest, and the conflict with Huwawa is anticipated in a threefold dream. The heroes defy the giant by felling cedars, and the conflict ensues, the details of which unfortunately are lost. Eventually Shamash intervenes, halting Huwawa with eight strong winds, and the giant submits to the heroes, who decapitate their enemy.

GILGAMESH SPURNS THE GODDESS ISHTAR

This exploit leads to the second, the suit of the goddess Ishtar for Gilgamesh, his repulse of her and the direful consequences. Ishtar's proposal to the hero clearly indicates her double character as a goddess of love and war:

Come, Gilgamesh, be thou my lover!
Do but grant me of thy fruit.
Thou shalt be my husband, and I will be thy wife.
I will harness for thee a chariot of lapis and gold,
Whose wheels are gold and whose horns are brass.
Thou shalt have storm-demons to hitch on for mighty mules.
In the fragrance of cedars thou shalt enter our house.
When our house thou enterest,
Threshold and dais shall kiss thy feet!
Humbled before thee shall be kings, lords and princes.
The yield of hills and plains they shall bring before thee as tribute.
Thy goats shall cast triplets, thy sheep twins,
Thy he-ass in lading shall surpass thy mule.
Thy chariot-horses shall be famed for racing,
Thine ox under yoke shall not have a rival.

Gilgamesh spurns the advances of the goddess, citing various instances from nature and mythology, where the love of the goddess had incited, eventually to degrade and destroy, like that of the ruthless Circe in the *Odyssey*. The 'shepherd-bird', in an allusion which is obscure, has momentarily enjoyed her love, and is thereafter condemned to perpetual lamentations, an explanatory myth accounting for the bird's cry '*kappi*' ('My wing'). A shepherd had been the object of her fatal love, at the end to be turned into a wolf, to be hounded by his own herdsmen and worried by his own dogs, like Actaeon so destroyed by Artemis in Greek mythology. There is an allusion to explanatory myth about the mole, which was regarded as the metamorphosis of another victim, the temple-gardener fatally loved by Ishtar. The momentary erotic ecstasy of the lion and the stallion are also contrasted with the downfall of the former in the hunt and the danger and fatigue of the war-stallion, perhaps an allusion to the first stage in the taming of the beasts by the use of a female as a decoy (see page 89). Ishtar's love had also excited the god of spring vegetation Tammuz, the counterpart of Greek Adonis in the seasonal nature-cult. But she was not able to save him from annual death, which was bewailed by her own votaries in a seasonal ritual that was widespread throughout the ancient Near East and the Mediterranean world, and is specifically mentioned in Ezekiel 8.14 and implied in Zechariah 12.11.

The motif of the repulse of the goddess of love is found also in Greek mythology in the myth of Artemis and Actaeon and in Canaanite mythology in the repulse of Anat by the prince Aqht in the Ras Shamra texts. There is another point of contact with the latter in that the goddess denounces the hero to the senior god of the pantheon and by threats secures his approval or help to take vengeance. Similarly, Ishtar, with the threat that she will break down the gates of the underworld and release the dead to swallow up the living, induces Anu to send a seven-year drought and famine, another common saga motif among the Canaanites and in the Old Testament, e.g. in the story of Joseph in Egypt (Genesis 4.54) and Elisha in Palestine (2 Kings 8.1). This particular vengeance on Gilgamesh is probably connected with the conception of the ancient king as the channel of divine blessing in nature, like rain-making African chiefs, who are tolerated as long as they are deemed effective. However that may be, the drought and famine are depicted as a redoubtable monster, the Bull of Heaven, the power of the plague-god Nergal. This was the god who was active in the intense heat of the sun at mid-day and in the summer solstice, the hot desert wind being his breath, which in one fragmentary passage is said to be alone sufficient to slay men in hundreds. The heroes, however, slay the Bull of Heaven, offering its heart to Gilgamesh's patron Shamash, and with a truly heroic, if ungallant, gesture, throw the hind-leg in Ishtar's face. So Gilgamesh and Enkidu return in triumph to Uruk, and in a greeting well known in the Old Testament, e.g. Exodus 15.20–21 (after the crossing of the Red Sea), they are welcomed by the antiphonal chanting of women, who play the harp to the theme suggested by the hero's boast:

Who is most splendid among the heroes?
Who is most glorious among men?

Gilgamesh is most splendid among the heroes,
Gilgamesh is most glorious among men.

The hero's boast, the prerogative of the ancient warrior, as a suggestion for a theme to the women welcoming home the warrior may explain the mention of the wives of the patriarch Lamech in Genesis 4.23–24:

Ada and Zillah, hear my voice,
Ye wives of Lamech, hearken to what I say;
I have slain a young man for wounding me,
A young man for striking me.
If Cain is avenged seven-fold,
Truly Lamech seventy-seven-fold.

THE DEATH OF ENKIDU

The Gilgamesh Legend in its extant version reaches its dramatic catastrophe with the death of Enkidu, which is foreshadowed by Gilgamesh's dream of a dispute in the celestial council. At the instance of Enlil, the executive of Anu, a life is claimed for the sacrilege in killing the Bull of Heaven, and Enkidu is stricken with mortal illness. He suffers 'one day, a second day' and so on to the conventional twelfth day of Mesopotamian legend, a reflection of the sexagesimal system which was the basis of Mesopotamian mathematics. This is the opportunity for the sage who composed the Legend to assess through the dying Enkidu the worth of human endeavour and aspiration after achievement and fame for its own sake as against the travail and physical suffering which they involve. To the ancient Mesopotamian as to the Hebrew in Old Testament times until the second century B.C., there was no prospect that he should after death 'rest from his labours' and his works should follow him. Enkidu knows that he is being led to:

Akkadian seal-impression (2340-2180 B.C.) depicting Gilgamesh's journey beyond the gates at the ends of the earth guarded by the doorkeepers. He met Utnapishtim, the survivor of the flood on whom the gods had conferred immortality, at the source of waters. British Museum.

. . . the House of Darkness,
The abode of Irkalla,
To the house which none leave who have entered it,
On the road from which there is no way back,
To the house wherein the dwellers are bereft of light,
Where dust is their fare and clay their food,
They are clothed like birds with wings for garments,
And see no light, residing in darkness.
In the House of Dust which I entered
I looked at rulers, their crowns put away;
I saw princes, those born to the crown,
Who had ruled the land from the days of yore.

This passage recalls Job 3.13–19:

I should have slept; then I should have been at rest
With kings and counsellors of the earth,
· · · · · ·
There the wicked cease from troubling,
And the weary are at rest,
There the prisoners are at ease together;
They hear not the voice of the task-master.
The small and the great are there,
And the slave is free from his master.

Enkidu's final word, however, declares that a death in action on some high enterprise is a blessing, and that had been the consolation of man up to this part of the text. But when death comes obscurely as the result of disease, the problem of human limitation weighs more heavily on the sage and his hero.

Gilgamesh mourns Enkidu, recalling his significance and exploits, as David recalled those of the dead Saul and Jonathan (2 Samuel 1.19–27):

The axe at my side, my hand's trust,
The dirk in my belt, the shield in front of me,
My festal robe, my richest trimming,
An evil demon rose up and robbed me!
O my younger friend, thou didst chase
The wild ass of the hills, the panther of the steppe!
Enkidu, my younger friend, thou who didst chase
The wild ass of the hills, the panther of the steppe!
We who have conquered all things,
Scaled the mountains,
Who seized the Bull and slew him,
Brought affliction on Huwawa, who dwelt in the cedar forest,
What, now, is this sleep that hath laid hold on thee?
Thou art benighted and canst not hear me!
But he lifts not up his eyes;
He touched his heart, but it does not beat,
Then he veiled his friend like a bride . . .
Storming over him like a lion,
Like a lioness deprived of her whelps,
He paces back and forth before the couch,
Pulling out his hair and strewing it . . .
Tearing off and throwing down his finery,
As though unclean . . .

Having presumably buried Enkidu and made funeral offerings, Gilgamesh turns earnestly to the quest, now no longer for fame but for life itself. Alone now, he undertakes long and arduous journeys beyond the bounds of human habitation to Utnapishtim, who had survived the Flood in Sumerian legend and had with his wife been granted eternal life at the remote 'outflowing of the rivers'. He meets with various obstacles, but is not deterred.

GILGAMESH SEEKS IMMORTALITY

First he arrives at the mountains on the rim of the world, where the frontier is guarded by Scorpion-men. Their chief endeavours to persuade Gilgamesh of the futility of his mission, but in vain. Eventually, after a long journey through the dark mountain-barrier visualised apparently to the north, where the fruits are semi-precious stones, he encounters by the sea, presumably the Mediterranean, a female named Siduri, which means in the non-Semitic Hurrian language of those regions 'young woman'. She is probably a minor deity, and is described as an ale-house keeper. At first alarmed at the stranger and barring him out, she proves true to her calling and is a ready confidante, and Gilgamesh tells her his trouble:

He who with me underwent all hardships—
Enkidu, whom I loved dearly,
Who with me underwent all hardships—
Enkidu has now gone to the fate of mankind!
Day and night I have wept over him.
I would not give him up for burial—
In case my friend should rise at my plaint—
Seven days and seven nights,
Until a worm fell out of his nose.
Since his passing I have not found life,
I have roamed like a hunter in the midst of the steppe.
O ale-wife, now that I have seen thy face,
Let me not see the death which I ever dread.

Her reply is to offer him the practical advice that he should forsake the vain quest for immortality and exploit the natural advantages of life and fulfil his natural desires:

Gilgamesh, whither rovest thou?
The life thou pursuest thou shalt not find.
When the gods created mankind,
Death for mankind they set aside,
Life in their own hands retaining.
Thou, Gilgamesh, let thy belly be full,
Make thou merry by day and by night.
Of each day make thou a feast of rejoicing,
Day and night dance thou and play!
Let thy garments be sparkling fresh,
Let thy head be washed; bathe thou in water.
Pay heed to the little one that holds on to thy hand,
Let thy spouse delight in thy bosom!
For this is the task of mankind.

But Gilgamesh persists in his quest and is not deterred by her warning that he must follow the sun's path to 'the waters of death', over which he must be ferried by the boatman Urshanabi, the Mesopotamian counterpart of the Greek Charon, the ferryman over the Styx.

On meeting Urshanabi, Gilgamesh answers the same question that Siduri had put to him with the same statement of his grief for the death of his friend and the same account of their exploits together and the death of Enkidu.

To his request to be ferried over, Urshanabi replies that Gilgamesh had, apparently inadvertently, destroyed certain stone amulets necessary for the voyage. Now he must provide twice-sixty stout punting-poles shod with ferrules. Such a large number was necessary since none might be used for more than one thrust and none of the waters of death must be touched by hand. After sailing a normal voyage of a month and a half in three days, they reached the waters of death, where the poles were brought into use. These were all used up, and the resourceful Gilgamesh was obliged to complete his voyage using his loincloth as a sail.

UTNAPISHTIM AND THE FLOOD

Utnapishtim sees him in the distance. The encounter is not actually described, but in a fragmentary passage the same questions are put and the same answers given as at Gilgamesh's meetings with Siduri and Urshanabi.

To Gilgamesh's request for eternal life, Utnapishtim's answer is not encouraging:

Do we build a house forever?
Do we seal contracts forever?
Do brothers divide shares forever?
Does hatred persist forever in the land?
Does the river forever raise up and bring on floods?
The dragon-fly leaves its husk
That its face might but glance at the face of the sun.
Since the days of yore there has been no permanence;
The resting of the dead, how alike they are!
Do they not compose a picture of death,
The commoner and the noble,
Once they are near to their fate.
The Anunnaki, the great gods, foregather;
Mammetum, maker of fate, with them the fate decrees:
Death and life they determine,
But of death, its days are not revealed.

Fragment of the Babylonian version of the flood narrative from the Gilgamesh legend in Akkadian cuneiform script. British Museum.

Questioned by Gilgamesh on how he had attained eternal life, which evidently means eternal quiescence, Utnapishtim recounts how he had survived the Flood. So, into the Gilgamesh epic there is worked the celebrated digression on the Flood, one version of the ancient Mesopotamian Flood-legend.

In this version no reason is given for the Deluge, unlike the versions in the Old Testament in which it is an instrument of God's moral judgment (Genesis 6.5–7 in the earlier Hebrew version of about the tenth century B.C., and Genesis 6.13 in the later version of about the sixth century B.C.). Another Akkadian myth, however, that of Atrahasis, the Exceeding Wise, which is an epithet of Utnapishtim, tells how the gods were troubled by the rapid increase of men and the noise that they made, disturbing the peace of the gods. Accordingly, famine is sent, and then the Flood, which seems from the fragmentary text to be a variant of that in the Gilgamesh Epic. Utnapishtim begins his narrative:

Shuruppak, a city which thou knowest,
And which on Euphrates' bank is situated,
That city was ancient, as were the gods within it,
When their heart led the great gods to produce the flood.

Cane-plaited hall in the marshes of southern Mesopotamia. It is the kind of 'reed-hut' to which the god Ea divulged the secret of the flood.

The counsel of the gods, however, was divulged by Ea, the god of water and wisdom, to Utnapishtim, the 'Man of Shuruppak', which probably signifies the king. The communication is said to be to the reed-hut, possibly one of those elaborate cane-plaited halls which are a feature of the Mesopotamian marshes at the present day and which probably served as a council chamber. And with the warning instructions are given to provide for survival in a large vessel:

Give up possessions, seek thou life.
Forswear worldly goods and keep the soul alive!
Aboard the ship take thou the seed of all living things.
The ship that thou shalt build,
Her dimensions shall be to measure.
Equal shall be her width and her length,
Like the Apsu that shalt ceil her.

The warning is not to be shared with the community at large. When questions are asked Utnapishtim is instructed to give a deceitful answer that he may no longer reside in the city owing to the weather-god Enlil, but must take to the water under the protection of Ea. He is, in fact, advised to lull his fellow-citizens into a false security.

The construction of the ark is then described:

With the first glow of dawn
The land was gathered about me
· · · · · · ·
The little ones carried bitumen,
While the grown ones brought all else that was needful.
On the fifth day I laid her framework,
One whole acre was her floor space,
Ten dozen cubits the height of each of her walls,
Ten dozen cubits each edge of the square deck.
I laid out the outside shape and joined her together,
I provided her with six decks,
Dividing her thus into seven parts.
Her floor plan I divided into nine parts.
I hammered water-plugs into her.
I saw to the punting-poles and laid in supplies.
Six sar-measures of bitumen I poured into the furnace,
Three sar of asphalt also I poured inside,
Three sar of oil the basket-bearers carried,
Aside from the one sar of oil which the calking consumed.
And the two sar of oil which the boatman stowed away.
Bullocks I slaughtered for the people,
And I killed sheep every day.
Must, red wine, oil and white wine
I gave the workmen to drink, as though river water,
That they might feast as on New Year's Day.
· · · · · · ·
On the seventh day the ship was completed.

Utnapishtim then loads on his possessions, with all his family including slaves and the craftsmen who had built the vessel, and beasts both wild and tame. Then, with the hatches battened down, she is handed over to the captain Puzur-Amurri.

The storm bursts in thunder and lightning, the province of Adad, the Amorite version of Sumerian Enlil and Canaanite Baal-Hadad, and the cosmic sluice-gates are opened:

With the first glow of dawn,
A black cloud rose up from the horizon.
Inside it Adad thunders,
While Shullat and Hanish go in front,
Moving as heralds over hill and plain.
Erragal tears out the posts;
Forth comes Ninurta and causes the dykes to overflow.
The Anunnaki lift up their torches,
Setting the land ablaze with their glare.
Consternation over Adad reaches to the heavens,
Who turned to blackness all that had been light.
The wide land was shattered like a pot;
For one day the storm wind blew,
Gathering speed as it blew, submerging the mountains,
Overtaking the people like a battle.
No one can see his fellow,
Nor can the people be recognised from heaven.

The fury of the flood they had sanctioned quells even the gods, who withdraw to the height of heaven, cowering 'like dogs crouched against the outer wall.'

The storm subsides 'on the seventh day' and Utnapishtim describes what he saw when he looked out:

I looked at the weather; stillness had set in,
And all of mankind had returned to clay.
The landscape was as level as a flat roof.
I opened a hatch, and light fell on my face.
I looked about for coastlines in the expanse of the sea;
Bowing low, I sat and wept.

Then Mount Nisir appears on which the vessel grounds and remains motionless 'one day, a second day,' etc., up to a sixth day. Then Utnapishtim describes his reconnaissance:

When the seventh day arrived,
I sent forth and set free a dove;
The dove went forth, but came back;
Since no resting-place for it was visible, she turned round.
Then I sent forth and set free a swallow.
The swallow went forth, but came back.
Since no resting-place for it was visible, she turned round.
Then I sent forth, and set free a raven.
The raven went forth and, seeing that the waters had diminished,
He eats, circles, caws, and turns not round.

Thereupon, Utnapishtim releases the animals and, like Noah (Genesis 8.20–21), offers savoury sacrifice:

Then I let out all to the four winds
And offered a sacrifice.
I poured out a libation on the top of the mountain.
Seven and seven cult-vessels I set up.
Upon their pot-stands I heaped cane, cedar-wood and myrtle.
The gods smelled the savour,
The gods smelled the sweet savour,
The gods crowded like flies about the sacrificer.

Nor is the Biblical motif of the rainbow (Genesis 9.9–21) lacking, a pledge that God will 'remember'. Ishtar, the life-giving goddess of love, swears by her jewelled necklace, that is the rainbow, that she would remember those awful days.

Enlil, the storm-god, who had brought about the Deluge, is angry at the betrayal of the secret, but he is calmed by the wise and tactful Ea, and finally confers immortality on Utnapishtim and his wife, convinced of the wisdom of Utnapishtim. But this immortality, in which Utnapishtim has affinity with the gods, is not to be shared with common humanity, so the two survivors of the Flood are to dwell henceforth at 'the outflow of the two rivers'. So ends the digression on the Flood in the Gilgamesh Epic.

GILGAMESH GIVES UP HIS QUEST

Gilgamesh's quest for immortality, however, does not yet end. At this point, the sage compiler of the epic turns to irony. Gilgamesh, who seeks so ardently after immortality, is challenged by Utnapishtim to hold out against sleep for 'six days, yea seven nights', and he fails, whereupon Utnapishtim jibs at the sleeping hero:

Behold this hero who seeks life!
Sleep fans him like a mist.

Ruthlessly, to convince Gilgamesh of his innate weakness, Utnapishtim has his wife bake a cake for every day Gilgamesh has slept. When finally he wakes, protesting that he had just dozed off, the evidence of seven cakes at various stages of freshness or staleness convinces him that his claim to immortality is preposterous.

The kindly Utnapishtim then prepares to send Gilgamesh home, but on the suggestion of his wife he takes pity on him and directs him in consolation to find a submarine plant which would at least rejuvenate him, as the name suggests, 'man-becomes-young-in-old-age'. Accordingly Gilgamesh ties heavy stones to his feet, dives down, and enduring the prickles of the plant, secures it, cuts the stones from his feet and finally emerges with the coveted plant.

Even this prize, however, was to be denied man. On his return, now on dry land, Gilgamesh comes to a well, and as he bathes, a serpent smells the plant and steals it, sloughing its old skin as it disappears as if in ridicule of Gilgamesh. Here an aetiological, or explanatory, myth is worked into the Gilgamesh legend to explain how the serpent seems able to renew its life whereas man for all his efforts cannot arrest the onset of age and decrepitude.

This concludes the theme of the Gilgamesh Legend in its Akkadian version, the final tablet being the translation of a Sumerian fragment from the saga-cycle of Gilgamesh, which is really an addendum with no relevance to the epic. It is the most complete work of its kind, not an unworthy predecessor of the *Odyssey*, of equal dramatic power and literary finish, but with the essentially philosophical theme in sharper focus. On the problem of the contrast between man's innate aspiration and his essential limitation the sage is neither pessimistic nor over-optimistic. The main endeavour of Gilgamesh is mildly ridiculed in his encounter with Utnapishtim and the sequel, when the serpent filches the plant of rejuvenation, and it is significant that Utnapishtim says nothing to recommend eternal life, which is apparently a life of interminable indolence; neither are the achievements of Gilgamesh minimised. The sage's conclusion realistically admits man's moral limitations and wisely advises him not to allow vain aspirations or futile regrets to divert him from his natural social duties and available enjoyments. This he expresses in the homely words of the ale-wife Siduri, and this is the philosophy of that other great realist, the Jewish sage in Ecclesiastes 9.7–10 some 1,500 years later:

Go, eat your bread with enjoyment,
And drink your wine with a merry heart;
For God has already approved what you do.
Let your garments be always white;
Let not oil be lacking on your head.
Enjoy life with the wife whom you love,
All the days of your vain life
Which he has given you under the sun.
Whatever your hand finds to do,
Do it with your might,
For there is no work or thought
Or knowledge or wisdom in Sheol
To which you are going.

The king in the ancient Near East moves in the orbit of the gods, and is often therefore the subject of mythology.

The King

In the Gilgamesh epic we have noticed that the king, though a heroic figure two-thirds divine and one-third human, is still supported by an assembly of elders. In the Sumerian epic fragment concerning the historical incident of his wars with Kish, his power is even limited by this assembly, whose influence was counteracted not by his own authority, but by a second assembly, that of the fighting men. Here are evident traces of a democratic constitution in southern Mesopotamia. In this 'theocratic communism' the city-state is the estate of the god, where kingship is an emergency expedient, instituted *ad hoc* and not visualised as necessarily permanent. But in the competition between rival city-states such situations tended to be protracted or recurrent with a consequent continuance in the authority of the king, which, however, he held as a commission from the Divine King. Even so, the king enjoyed a peculiar blessing, which in the conception of the ancient Near East was shared by all about him, especially members of his own family, who were thus the most likely persons to succeed him if the situation demanded it, in spite of the fact that theoretically the kingship was a temporary expedient. The transmission of authority from an effective ruler to one of his own family, who had the natural advantages of association with his father, but had not been called to office, confronted Sumerians and Semites in ancient Mesopotamia and elsewhere in the ancient Near East with a problem, the reality of which is indicated by the deliberate attempts to authenticate the succession.

THE MYTH OF ETANA

The question of succession seems to us to be the subject of the myth of Etana, who is known from ancient Sumerian kinglists as one of the dynasty of Kish after the Flood. The myth, transmitted in Akkadian fragments from various ages in Babylon and Assyria, begins before the institution of kingship when

The black-headed people, in all, had not set up a king,
. . . . . .

There being no counselling (i.e. planning) for the people of the earth.

Then, it is stated, 'kingship descended from heaven'.

The late Assyrian version (seventh century B.C.) states that Enlil searches the land for a king. The fragmentary text does not say that the king was Etana, but as he is the hero of the sequel, this is virtually certain. The myth now relates, with the prolix verbal repetition of epic style, the initial friendship of the eagle and the serpent, which is disrupted by the treachery of the eagle in making a meal of the serpent's young. In requital for this, it is maimed and consigned to a pit by the serpent, but is healed by Etana to carry him up to the sky. The relevance of the episode of the eagle and the serpent is obscure and does not concern us. The object of Etana's flight, however, is significant. It is to secure the plant of birth, that his 'burden' or disability may be removed and 'a name' be produced for him. This indicates the problem of dynastic succession, which is also the theme of the two royal legends among the Canaanite Ras Shamra texts.

In the fragmentary state of the text the result of Etana's quest is uncertain. According to one fragment Etana arrives on his eagle at the celestial gate and does obeisance to Anu, Enlil and Ea, but the rest is lost. According to another

fragment Etana's nerve fails him before he reaches heaven, and he plunges back to the earth, at which point the tablet breaks off short. From the recurrence of the motif of Etana's flight on cylinder seals, H. Frankfort concludes that the mission was successful, as only successful exploits were so recorded. If this conjecture is correct the myth of Etana's quest for the plant of birth may have been used to support dynastic claims. If, on the other hand, the evidence of actual texts is to be followed, it may mark a protest against hereditary monarchy in favour of the old Sumerian ideal of primitive democracy.

This consciousness of the king's limitation before the gods characterises the conception of kingship in Mesopotamia as distinct from Egypt, where the Pharaoh was regarded as the incarnation of the sun-god Re, being united at his death with the fertility-god Osiris. Only exceptionally did the Mesopotamian king claim the status of the god, though cases are known, most notably the imperialist Naram-sin, who is depicted with the horned headdress of a god, scaled out of all proportion to his soldiers on a victory stele.

In view of the problem of royal accession or succession as a practical rule in contrast to ideal democracy, it is significant that ancient Mesopotamian kings were at pains to accentuate their status either as 'envisaged' by a god

or 'called by name', as Cyrus of Persia claimed to be in his record of his conquest of Babylon. That signified that the king was destined by the god to play a definite part in the divine purpose. Thus Hammurabi (about 1700 B.C.) was 'looked upon' by Shamash, the sun-god, and 'called by Anu and Enlil to establish justice in the community', an expression of which is his famous law code. The king may claim to be designated from his mother's womb, as did Nabona'id, the last king of the Aramaean Dynasty of Babylon. Or he may claim to be otherwise invested with power by the gods. This special divine designation may be denoted by oracle, as Esarhaddon (680–669 B.C.) claimed, stating that, though a younger son of Sennacherib, he was designated to succeed by oracles from Shamash and Adad. It was evidently a regular Assyrian practice to designate the heir-apparent and invest him as co-regent, a very practical expedient in a polygamous society, where a king's prestige was enhanced by the size of his harem, and one which was occasionally followed in Israel, certainly in the case of Solomon (1 Kings 1). We shall see just such a prophetic oracle authenticating the adoption of Hezekiah as heir-apparent and co-regent of King Ahaz of Judah in 729 B.C. in Isaiah 9.2–7. We shall study this later in the context of mythology in the Bible, particularly in the context of the ideology of kingship as the background of Messianic hopes.

THE LEGEND OF SARGON OF AKKAD

The problem of royal accession is accentuated in the case of a *nouveau venu*, either one who was called to meet an emergency or, more often, a man of ambition and action who rose by his own merits or resolution. Then the claim might be made to divine election and preservation in spite of obscure origin. The most notable instance is the legend of Sargon of Akkad, or Agade, probably the first great imperialist in history. In three extant fragments from

Northern Mesopotamian seal-impression depicting the king before the tree of life under the characteristic winged disc of the god Ashur. The lions may symbolise the fertility-goddess Ishtar. Staatliche Museen, Berlin.

the late Assyrian period Sargon claims to have been the son of an *enitum*, that is, a female devotee. The *enitum* was originally the bride of the god, for whom the king or chief-priest officiated, in the fertility rites of the sacred marriage. As such, she was sacrosanct, at least in the period of Sargon, though possibly by that time (2242–2186 B.C.) the status of *enitum* applied to a number of female devotees, all of whom were forbidden intercourse with ordinary male laymen. This would explain the secret birth of Sargon, which strangely recalls the story of Moses' origin, the tradition of which it may have influenced:

My mother, an *enitum*, conceived me; in secret she bore me,
She set me in a basket of rushes, with bitumen she sealed my lid,
She cast me into the river, which rose not over me,
The river bore me up and carried me to Akki, the drawer of water.
Akki, the drawer of water, lifted me out as he dipped his bucket.
Akki, the drawer of water, took me as his son and reared me,
Akki, the drawer of water, appointed me as his gardener.
While I was a gardener, Ishtar granted me her love,
And for four and . . . years I exercised kingship,
The black-headed people I ruled, I governed.

Then follows a summary account of his conquests.

After his rescue Sargon seems to have become attached to a temple in the capacity of gardener, whatever that implied. His admittance in this role to the love of Ishtar is tantalisingly obscure. One is tempted to think of rites of imitative magic in the fertility cult where a king consummated a sacred marriage with a priestess who played the role of the fertility goddess Ishtar (see above, page 22). Sargon's elevation may have been due to the choice of the chief priestess in Agade. As Sargon is known to have begun his political career as vizier of the King of Kish, this might represent an expedient of local politics in the emancipation from the dominion of Kish.

Assyrian seal-impression (ninth or eighth century B.C.) depicting the tree of life flanked by two griffin-genii and two caprids, and the fertility-goddess Ishtar characterised by her lion.

Right: bronze statuette covered with gold foil of a worshipper named Lunanna, who declares that he is praying 'for the life of Hummurabi King of Babylon [fl. 1700 B.C.] to his god Amurru'. Louvre.

Opposite: a statuette of a worshipper, probably the king as the worshipper *par excellence*, presenting a sacrifice. Louvre.

Seal-impression (*c.* 3000 B.C.) depicting the king feeding two caprids from branches of the tree of life. Ishtar's looped reed-bundle is a significant feature. Staatliche Museen, Berlin.

THE KING'S SOCIAL RESPONSIBILITY

The Mesopotamian king, thus established, is not allowed to forget his divine commission. In the annual ritual of the spring New Year festival in Babylon he gives up office, to receive it again from the priest of the god Marduk after rites of humiliation and a negative confession. Hammurabi in the prelude to his law code acknowledges his divine commission to uphold justice, and a certain astrologer in his reply to an Assyrian king reminds him that he is the representative of man and the image of God in protection of the community. In justice to the ancient kings in Mesopotamia it must be admitted that this onus of royalty was seriously assumed. Hence kings were at pains, like Hammurabi, to emphasise that they had succeeded in the integration of society and had secured the interests and rights of each class and individual in what was essentially a religious community.

When the king fulfilled this social responsibility, the country enjoyed well-being, Akkadian *shulmu*, Hebrew *shalom*, one aspect only of which is 'peace'. Thus Ashurbanipal claims:

'After Ashur, Sin, Shamash, Adad, Bel, Nabu, Ishtar of Nineveh, queen of Kidmuri, Ishtar of Arbela, Urta, Nergal and Nusku, had caused me to take my seat joyfully upon the throne of my father who begot me, Adad sent his rains, Ea opened his fountains, the grain grew five cubits tall in the stalk, the ear was five-sixths of a cubit long; heavy crops and a plenteous yield made the fields continuously luxuriant, the orchards yielded a rich harvest, the cattle successfully brought forth their young. In my reign there was fullness to overflowing, in my years there was plenteous abundance.'

The same conjunction of justice according to the will of God and material well-being is familiar in the Hebrew ideology of kingship, of which perhaps the best expression is Psalm 72.

The Assyrian King Ashurnasirpal II (883-859 B.C.) and his vice-regent (?), to whom two genii communicate fertility. They are depicted standing by the tree of life under the winged disc of the god Ashur. British Museum.

In Ashurbanipal's inscription just cited the hyperbole is obvious and is reminiscent of the later claim by the Pharisees that when the Pharisaic Rabbi Simon ben Shetach influenced affairs of state under Queen Shelom-Zion (Greek Salome), also called Alexandra (75–67 B.C.),

'. . . corns of wheat were as large as kidneys, the barley corns as large as olives, and the lentils like golden denarii.'

In the Mesopotamian royal inscriptions there is more than mere hyperbole. The king is praised extravagantly because he is the temporal guarantee of God's order in nature as well as in society. Just as Enlil or Marduk in Babylon, and Ashur in Assyria, as the executors of the celestial rule and order were protagonists in the sacramental celebration of creation in the New Year festival, so the accession of the king is in itself an expression of the assertion of the celestial rule and order. Thus, in the Assyrian variation of the New Year festival, after the symbolic victory of Ashur over the forces of Chaos, the king rode in triumph in the chariot of the god to the banqueting-hall to the acclamation of 'Ashur is King'. So also creation, which was the visible token of God's assertion of celestial government, was expected in consequence of the king's accession, and such prosperity as might be recorded was described in imagery which reflected creation. This is most familiar to us in the vivid imagery of the golden age of preternatural peace and phenomenal fertility in Isaiah 11.1–9. This passage, originally probably relevant to the accession of the king, was later associated with the coming of the Messiah of Jewish eschatological hope, and is the background of the miracles affecting the well-being of men in the mission of Jesus Christ the Messiah in the realisation of the reign of God.

The king as the medium of fertility watering the tree of life before the sun-god Shamash, from the Chaldaean period in Babylon (seventh or sixth century B.C.). Louvre.

THE TREE OF LIFE

To the Mesopotamian no less than to Israel the king was 'the breath of our nostrils' (Lamentations 4.20). In fact, this expression was used long before the fall of Jerusalem by King Ishme-Dagan of Isin (1884–1865 B.C.), who claims that he had been divinely appointed 'to guard the lifebreath of all lands . . .'; and Shulgi of the Third Dynasty of Ur (2026–1979) describes himself as 'a date-palm planted beside a watercourse'.

The imagery of the last reference is significant, referring probably to the association of the king with 'The Tree of Life', which is familiar in literature and art in Mesopotamia, Canaan and Israel, with local variations. Thus on a seal from Warka, ancient Uruk, the city of Gilgamesh, the king offers two fruitful branches to two caprids, which reach up to feed. The panel is significantly flanked by symbols of the fertility-goddess Ishtar, who may thus be symbolised by the sacred tree. The king as the medium of fertility was also expressed by the conception of the 'sacred marriage' with a priestess representing the mother-goddess. Thus Ishme-Dagan alludes to a 'sacred marriage' in the New Year festival, and in another text states:

I am he whom Inanna, Queen of heaven and earth, has chosen for her beloved husband.

This conception of the king as the medium of fertility through the fertility-goddess is expressed in Assyrian sculpture, where the king is touched by a protective genius with a cone dipped in some fertility substance, either pollen or oil, such as is usual to fertilise trees. The fertility is communicated by the king to a stylised version of the Tree of Life.

59

Right: bronze head of Sargon of Akkad (2241-2186 B.C.), the first great imperialist in world history. Iraq Museum.

Below: mural painting of the investiture of an Amorite king of Mari (c. 1900-1700 B.C.), with the tree of life and four streams issuing from one well-head, as in the picture of the garden of Eden in Genesis 2.9-10. Compare Genesis 3.24 for the conception of cherubim guarding the tree of life. Louvre.

Opposite: the Tree of Life motif from the 'royal' graves at Ur (c. 2700-2500 B.C.), popularly, but wrongly, taken as the prototype of the 'ram caught in a thicket by the horns', a forced parallel with Genesis 22.13. British Museum.

The motif of the Warka seal with the two caprids reaching up to the life-giving fruit is probably found also in the figurine of the 'ram caught in a thicket' from the royal graves of Ur (*c*. 2700–2500 B.C.). On the lid of an ivory cosmetic casket from Minet al-Beida near Ras Shamra in the fourteenth century the mother-goddess herself occupies the place of the tree between two rampant caprids to which she offers ears of corn. This seems to indicate finally the explanation of the Biblical references to the *'asherah* as a natural or stylised tree in the fertility cult. This was the symbol of the mother-goddess, now known from the Ras Shamra texts as Asherah, the counterpart of Mesopotamian Ishtar, or Inanna.

The Tree of Life in various stylised forms is known as a distinctive feature of palace architecture and ornamentation. It is found, for instance, in the proto-Ionic capitals from columns in palaces in Jerusalem, Samaria, Hazor, and Ramat Rahel between Jerusalem and Bethlehem, and on an ivory relief

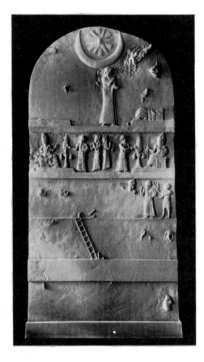

Stele of Urnammu of Ur (2022-2004 B.C.) watering the Tree of Life before Shamash the sun-god, distinguished by the measuring-line and the rod of justice. The tradition of Man (Hebrew 'adam) the cultivator of the Garden of Eden is a version of this motif in the royal ideology of Mesopotamia. The lower register depicts the king inaugurating the building of a temple to the moon-god Nannur, whose emblem surmounts the sculpture. University of Pennsylvania Museum.

Right: genii fertilising the Tree of Life, flanked by a stylised version of the tree. Phoenician ivory from a bed at Nimrud (eighth or seventh century B.C.). Compare the ivory from the royal couch at Ugarit (page 90). British Museum.

of the royal couch in the palace at Ras Shamra, where it is combined with the Egyptian motif of a flourishing lotus. It is thus at once significant as a pledge of prosperity to the king and as a symbol of his potency in channelling prosperity to the community.

The significance of the king as the divine nominee through whom came all blessings is admirably illustrated in a remarkable mural painting from the Amorite palace of Mari on the Euphrates. This depicts the king's investiture by the goddess Ishtar, distinguished by her lion, the goddess potent in love and war. The stylised palm-tree, the Tree of Life, is represented in duplicate for the sake of symmetry in the composition of the picture, and it is guarded by two winged sphinx-figures, Hebrew 'cherubim'. They recall the Biblical tradition of the cherubim guarding access to the tree of life in Genesis 3.24. In the lower panels of this picture, the fertility theme is sustained by four streams issuing from each of two jars. A plant, or young tree, grows in each jar, again suggesting the Biblical motif of the four streams from the one fountainhead in the Garden of Eden (Genesis 2.10–14).

Alabaster relief from the palace of Ashurbanipal (668-626 B.C.) at Nineveh depicting the king and queen feasting in an arbour. They hold the plant of life and well-being, which may be the origin of the flower as the specific emblem of consecration of kings and later high-priests (Exodus 39.30) in Israel. British Museum.

Below left: Gudea of Lagash (c.2275-2260 B.C.) introduced by the god Ningizzidu and another to a high god, probably the fertility-goddess Inanna, called also Ishtar. The king, as a medium of fertility, bears a branch from the Tree of Life. From a stele at Tello.

Above: King Gudea of Lagash (c. 2275-2260 B.C.), dispenser of the never-failing water, in the same attitude as the fertility-goddess Ishtar (page 30). Louvre.

The motif of the lower register of the Mari panel recurs in royal sculptures where the king waters the plant in a tall pot-stand before a god. The motif also recurs in inscriptions where the king claims to be the gardener in the garden of God, with the duty of watering the Plant of Life. Specifically this may refer to the role of the king in the cult of Tammuz, who was evidently symbolised by the plant. A variant of this motif is the king as dispenser of the Water of Life, which is strikingly expressed in the statue of Gudea of Lagash pouring a never-failing stream of water from a jar. The jar is held in a peculiar position which suggests the saying of Jesus – 'out of his belly shall flow rivers of living water' (John 7.38). This position is exactly reproduced in the sculpture of the fertility-goddess with the jar from Mari. In the king as gardener of the god tending the Plant of Life, we have surely the original of primordial man (Hebrew 'adam), the image of God, in the Garden of Eden, with its Tree of Life. With this very suggestive figure there is bound up the responsibility of the king in the ancient Near East, the Jewish and Christian theology of man in the image of God, and the ideology of the Messiah.

CANAAN

Syria and Palestine, Biblical Canaan, were part of the higher regions as distinct from the great river valleys of the Near East. Growth depended chiefly on seasonal rain rather than on large-scale irrigation. The country's initial asset was wild wheat, from which cereal cultivation developed. There is evidence of harvesting of such a crop in serrated pieces of flint sickle-blades from the Mesolithic period in Palestine (about 10,000–7,500 B.C.).

THE LAND

Farming communities settled in small units according to the configuration of the land, in contrast to the relatively large concentration of population in southern Mesopotamia after the coming of the Sumerians. The land rises abruptly from the coastal plain from just north of Gaza in southern Palestine to the Gulf of Alexandretta in northern Syria, occasionally reaching over 6,000 feet in the Lebanon. The prevailing wind occasioned by the air from the Mediterranean to the inland deserts comes laden with moisture, which, quickly forced upwards to a great height, condenses in heavy rain in winter and dew in summer. The summer dew is specially noticed in the Canaanite texts from Ras Shamra and in the Old Testament, and can be as heavy as a fine drizzle of rain. Here drainage was natural and never a problem as in southern Mesopotamia. The local problem was rather erosion of soil on the hillsides which are unprotected by turf. Here, however, natural terraces of limestone may halt erosion and encourage artificial terracing by dry stones, which are picked out of the plots of earth during cultivation. On the hillsides are grown vines and olives, which, with natural pine and cedar forests in the Lebanon and Amanus, were the main products of the land. Moreover, soil which is eroded builds up fertile pockets of earth and even considerable plains. Such cultivable land was regarded as 'Baal's land', that is to say, land where cultivation depends on the activity of the god manifest in the autumn and winter rains. These rains are heralded by thunder, and 'the lord' (Baal) was known to the Canaanites by his proper name Hadad, 'the Thunderer', or Rimmon, which means the same. The term 'Baal-land' as distinct from irrigated land has survived in Muslim law in tax assessment for poor relief.

The heavy seasonal rains, permeating the porous limestone of which the country largely consists, collect underground and replenish small but fairly plentiful springs, which serve for irrigation of relatively small areas without necessitating large-scale co-operation as in the urban communities of southern Mesopotamia. The local independence of communities in Canaan precluded political development beyond very small city-states. The result was a less sophisticated culture than in Mesopotamia, and certainly a much less complicated relationship with the gods on whom the natives relied for the satisfaction of their relatively modest needs. Social relationships, too, were relatively uncomplicated, being fundamentally related to the common ethic of fairly clearly defined tribal groups, by which the population was continually replenished from the Arabian steppe.

CULTURAL DEVELOPMENT

Throughout this region the metropolises of local culture were places which stood in fertile, well-watered terrain on vital trade-routes. These routes traversed this corridor between the two great seats of civilisation and empire in antiquity, Mesopotamia and Egypt. Certain inland cities of Canaan, such as Jericho, Bethshan, Megiddo, and Hazor in Palestine and Damascus and

Previous page: one of the few remaining stands of cedar in Lebanon, which was heavily drawn on by Egypt and Mesopotamian powers, and supplied cedar for Solomon's Temple. The great timber port was Byblos.

Top: the tell (ruin-mound) of Hama with remains from the third millennium B.C. to the seventh century A.D. in the valley of the Orontes in Syria.

Centre: the modern town of Tyre in Lebanon, which was on a rocky offshore island. This was reached by a siege-mole constructed by Alexander the Great in 332 B.C., which sanded up to form the present peninsula.

Bottom: the coast and mountains of Lebanon. The rocky indented coast afforded natural harbours for sea-faring, to which the Phoenicians or Canaanites turned because of the limitations of the narrow coastal plain.

Aleppo in Syria, had considerable importance. But the most sophisticated centres of Canaanite culture, which influenced the whole area, were the cities on the Syrian coast, later known as Phoenicia, such as Tyre, Sidon, Beirut, Byblos, Arad and notably Ugarit (modern Ras Shamra). Ugarit had contacts by sea with many peoples in the second millennium B.C.

These foreign contacts introduced certain foreign influences in culture and religion, which will be noted in our study of Canaanite mythology. The influence at Ras Shamra and Byblos, the great timber port of the Lebanon, was mainly Egyptian, though that was rather in secular culture than religion. But in mythology and the ideology of kingship the greater affinity is with Mesopotamia, with the Semitic element through which the Canaanites shared ultimately a common heritage in the northern Arabian steppe.

The intermediate situation of Canaan and the local isolation and limited political and economic development encouraged assimilation rather than initiative. But this very limitation led to one most significant invention, which characteristically was stimulated by the achievements of the inhabitants of Mesopotamia and Egypt, namely the development of the alphabet. Experiments were made to transform the Akkadian cuneiform script, with which the Mesopotamians wrote on clay tablets, and the Egyptian hieroglyphics from complicated combinations of consonants and vowels (syllabic script) to an alphabet consisting only of consonants. Such an alphabet, as in modern Arabic and Hebrew, can prove practically quite adequate even without vowels. Two successful experiments attained this end. One was the cuneiform alphabet, best known from Ras Shamra since the initial discovery of literary texts there in 1929; the other was the immediate ancestor of the Hebrew, and incidentally of the Greek and Latin, alphabets. This linear script was used to record certain epitaphs in royal graves in Byblos from the end of the second millennium B.C. and for inscriptions from Aramaean kingdoms of the interior of Syria from the eighth century B.C., as well as later Phoenician inscriptions from the coastal cities. But the fuller records, which we know from an Egyptian inscription were kept at Byblos on papyrus imported from Egypt, would soon perish in the humidity of the soil in the Levant. At Ras Shamra, however, the much clumsier cuneiform was written on clay tablets, which when dried or even baked are, with normal use, virtually indestructible. These tablets, beyond the most extravagant hopes of scholars before 1930, are our sources for the mythology of Canaan in the fourteenth century B.C.

Religion

Until 1929 our impression of Canaanite religion was distorted by the fulmination of Hebrew prophets and reformers at 'the abominations of the Canaanites'. They objected to the artless cult of the power of providence in nature involving rites of imitative magic such as ritual prostitution to prompt the fertility of flock and field and amulets of the fertility-goddess in her various manifestations, the local counterparts of Mesopotamian Inanna or Ishtar. A neutral source is a work on the Syrian Goddess by Lucian of Samosata about A.D. 150, but this is limited to a local fertility cult of this goddess with that of Adonis, the Syrian Tammuz. A more comprehensive and systematic account, which suggests the philosophic rationalisation of early Mesopotamian myths, as in *enuma elish*, was produced by Philo of Byblos (about A.D. 100), allegedly on the basis of a twelfth-century work. While the first-hand material from Ras Shamra indicates that there was a substantial substratum of genuine nature-religion in Philo's account, its value is impaired by Philo's determination to force ancient Canaanite religion into the mould of a Greek philosophic system. Archaeology has now supplied first-hand evidence in temples and cult-objects and, most significantly, actual Canaanite texts, notably those from Ras Shamra.

CANAANITE TEXTS

A significant discovery of this nature consisted of two lots of texts from Egypt which were used in rites of execration of the Pharaoh's enemies from about 1850 to 1800 B.C. These texts name Amorite chiefs of Palestine and southern Syria and the names disclose the identity and nature of their gods. The earlier texts indicate the gods of tribesmen, who are regarded as kinsmen and so impose social obligations; the later texts indicate the development of settled communities worshipping the local fertility-god Baal-Hadad.

With the Ras Shamra texts from the fourteenth century B.C., comprising ritual texts, myths and legends relating to ancient kings and the gods, we have a reasonably full documentation of Canaanite religion.

The Canaanites evidently knew nothing of the elaborate pantheon and cosmogony of the Mesopotamians, which probably reflects the relative simplicity of their lives. Their interest was not to correlate and explain the various forces of nature and society in all the complexity of harmony and tension, but to declare their dependence on the gods and to placate them.

EL, THE CHIEF GOD

Corresponding to Anu in Mesopotamia, the king paramount in the celestial court was El ('God'), who gives his sanction to all decisions among the gods affecting nature and society. He is father of the divine family and president of the divine assembly on the 'mount of assembly', the equivalent of Hebrew *har mô'ed*, which became through the Greek transliteration *Armageddon*. In Canaanite mythology he is known as 'the Bull', symbolising his strength and creative force, and is probably represented in the elderly god who is blessing a worshipper on a limestone sculpture from Ras Shamra. In the myths he is termed 'Creator of Created Things', but he is generally depicted as sitting aloof and indeed remote, enthroned at 'the outflowing of the (two) streams'. This recalls the Biblical Garden of Eden, from which a river flowed to form the four rivers, Tigris, Euphrates, Gihon and Pishon. The Bible also has the mythological theme of the river flowing from under the throne of God in Jerusalem (Ezekiel 47.1–12; Psalms 46.4).

Opposite: terracotta moulded plaques of the nude fertility-goddess Astarte with the coiffure of her Egyptian counterpart Hathor. The lotus symbols and fertility organs are emphasised. The plaques were possibly amulets received in return for the payment of vows to the goddess. Archaeological Museum, Jerusalem.

Left: gold pendants with motif of Astarte naturalistic or stylised from Ras Shamra, c 1300 B.C. National Museum, Aleppo.

Below: stele from Ras Shamra depicting a god, perhaps El, on his throne, with footstool, receiving an offering and blessing a worshipper, who is probably the king. National Museum, Aleppo.

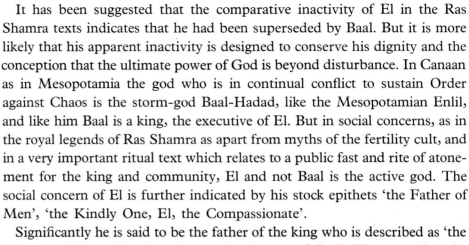

Life-sized sculpture of Baal-Hadad from his temple at Ras Shamra (*c.* 2000 B.C.), with mace and spear. The haft of the spear is a tree, probably a cedar, as indicated in a seal and in the Baal myth from Ras Shamra. The undulating lines under him may be mountains or, more probably, the clouds and water of the earth, by his mastery of which Baal in the myth of Ras Shamra signalises his kingship. The small figure in front of him possibly depicts the king, the executive of Baal the divine king. Louvre.

It has been suggested that the comparative inactivity of El in the Ras Shamra texts indicates that he had been superseded by Baal. But it is more likely that his apparent inactivity is designed to conserve his dignity and the conception that the ultimate power of God is beyond disturbance. In Canaan as in Mesopotamia the god who is in continual conflict to sustain Order against Chaos is the storm-god Baal-Hadad, like the Mesopotamian Enlil, and like him Baal is a king, the executive of El. But in social concerns, as in the royal legends of Ras Shamra as apart from myths of the fertility cult, and in a very important ritual text which relates to a public fast and rite of atonement for the king and community, El and not Baal is the active god. The social concern of El is further indicated by his stock epithets 'the Father of Men', 'the Kindly One, El, the Compassionate'.

Significantly he is said to be the father of the king who is described as 'the Servant of El', as King David was 'the Servant of God'. This describes the status of the king as the executive of the will of the divine king. This duty is a privilege as well as a burden.

BAAL, THE EXECUTIVE OF THE HEAVENLY COURT

Baal on the other hand, like Enlil, Adad, Marduk, and Ashur in Mesopotamia, is the divine executive of the heavenly court, the kingship of God made effective, particularly in nature. Like Enlil and his Mesopotamian variations, Baal-Hadad is active in the storms of rain, thunder, and lightning in winter, and the lightning is his weapon, of which he boasts in a certain mythological text. Like Enlil, or Adad, his cult-animal is the bull, the horns of which he wears on his helmet. Like his Mesopotamian counterparts, he champions the divine Order against the menace of Chaos, at one time typified as the unruly waters, at another as the drought and sterility of the Syrian summer. He thus represents the royal power and authority of God not aloof and beyond the menace of evil, but continually menaced yet triumphant. In agreement with this conception of the dynamic authority of God, he is represented in sculpture and figurines as a striding warrior in a short kilt with a dagger at his belt, ready for action and helmeted. He brandishes a mace and wields a spear, which in token of his fertilising power is hafted with a branching tree. His stock epithets are 'Baal the Mighty' and 'He who Mounts the Clouds', which is almost exactly used as an epithet of God as the Divine King in Old Testament liturgies. His activity, however, is not so wide as that of Enlil, for he is limited to the sphere of nature.

He is identified with the vegetation he promotes, a character expressed by his designation 'son of Dagan', i.e. the corn-god, who also had a temple alongside that of Baal on the summit of the city of Ras Shamra. He is, like Mesopotamian Tammuz, a dying and rising god, whose vicissitudes on earth and in the underworld may be related to the course of the agricultural year in rites connected with the myth of Baal in his conflict with Death, or Sterility. In this myth the role of Anat, his sister, is significant, recalling that of Ishtar in Mesopotamia in the myth and ritual associated with Tammuz.

GODDESSES

El's female counterpart in the Ras Shamra myths is the mother-goddess Asherah, who is more actively engaged in the myth of the fertility cult concerning Baal's conflict with Sterility. In particular, she intercedes with El to sanction a temple for Baal in token of his victory over the power of Chaos

Top left: stele from Balua in Moab, depicting an ancient ruler of Moab standing between Baal, distinguished by his horned helmet, and the fertility and war-goddess Anat, wearing her headdress with ostrich plumes of Osiris (twelfth or eleventh century B.C.). Archaeological Museum, Jerusalem.

Top right: Syrian sculpture of a calf, or bull, possibly an enthroned figure of Baal-Hadad with dagger at belt and wearing the head of his cult-animal the bull. Damascus Museum.

Bottom left: the god of the sea in Egyptian sculpture characterised by the zigzag motif, the Egyptian hieroglyph for 'water'. Cairo Museum.

Below: bronze figurine of a Canaanite god, probably Baal (c. 1300 B.C.). British Museum.

and of his royal authority. This is the goddess represented in the position of the tree of life between the animals, which depend on her for sustenance. Hence derives the name of the sacred emblem, the stylisation of the tree of life, which is called the *asherah* in the Old Testament. (In the Authorised Version, it is called 'the grove'.)

The goddess peculiarly associated with Baal is Anat, like Ishtar a goddess of love and war. She complements Baal, abetting him in his conflict and vindicating him when he succumbs, possibly reflecting the role of women at the critical seasons of transition in popular religion or when the order of the gods is temporarily in eclipse. Related to such phases is certainly the weeping of the women in Jerusalem for Tammuz (Ezekiel 8.14) and possibly the lamentations of the maidens of Israel, which may be only secondarily related to the mourning for Jephthah's daughter (Judges 11.39–40).

The goddess other than Asherah associated with the fertility cult in Canaan in the Old Testament is Astarte, the Canaanite version of the name Ishtar. But she plays a minor role in the Ras Shamra texts, her functions being taken over by Anat. In fact in Canaan there is a tendency for the distinctive functions of the three goddesses to fuse together, as we see clearly from the Egyptian rendering of the fertility-goddess in a sculpture from the nineteenth dynasty. It depicts the mother-goddess named Qodshu ('Holiness') naked between the Egyptian fertility-god Min and the Canaanite Reshef, the god with power of life or death. The goddess stands on a lion, the cult-animal of Mesopotamian Ishtar, and she is represented on the lower register and actually named Anat.

MINOR DEITIES

There are other minor deities in the religion of Canaan and particularly in the Ras Shamra texts. First there is Yamm the Sea, the adversary of Baal as the champion of Order against Chaos. Yamm is called 'Prince Sea and Ocean Current the Ruler', and is the local counterpart of Mesopotamian Tiamat in Marduk's battle on behalf of the divine Order in the myth of the Babylonian New Year festival. Then in the myth which relates Baal's vicissitudes as a dying and rising god in the Canaanite New Year festival his adversary is Mot, Death or Sterility, called in one text Death-and-Dissolution. Mot reigns in the underworld amid ruin and darkness, and there he is Death. As the adversary to whom Baal eventually succumbs in the summer heat he is Sterility. In the myth of his conflict with Baal, however, he is destroyed by Baal's sister and avenger Anat. The fact that Mot is still alive to challenge Baal to a critical combat later in the text is clear evidence that in such texts relating to seasonal rituals we must not try to find the absolute logical sequence of an independent narrative.

We shall also encounter in the Baal myth minor figures such as Baal's three 'girls', daughters or concubines, who are nymphs of Dew, Rain and Fatness; his messengers Vine and Field, and similar attendants of other gods, who always occur in pairs. They also include the divine craftsman, the Skilful and Percipient One, patron of craftsmanship and magic. Local tradition preserves a historical reminiscence of the influence of Egypt on Canaanite culture in these coastal regions in associating him with *hgkpt* ('the country of Ptah'), that is the city of Memphis at the apex of the Delta, the cult-centre of Ptah and patron of the mechanical arts. It is the Skilful and

Left: the Canaanite fertility-goddess in Egyptian sculpture (*c.* 1300 B.C.), named Qodshu, possibly 'the sacred prostitute' *par excellence*, indicated by the lion as Astarte. Her fertility function is indicated by the lotus she proffers to the Egyptian fertility-god Min. She proffers serpents to Reshef, the Canaanite god. British Museum.

Below: Mycenaean ivory lid of an unguent box from the shore settlement by Ras Shamra (*c.* 1300 B.C.). It depicts the mother-goddess Ashera seated between two caprids to which she offers ears of corn. She thus occupies the place of the tree of life. Louvre.

Percipient One who supplies Baal with his weapons to overcome 'Prince Sea, even Ocean Current the Ruler'. Athtar is also mentioned in the Baal myth. He was originally the god manifest in the Venus-star and venerated by tribesmen in the Syrian desert, but after the settlement in Canaan he was a god associated with irrigation (the Arabic word *'athara* means 'to irrigate') and a sorry substitute for Baal-Hadad in his temporary eclipse.

A clear reminiscence of the cult of the Venus-star in its twin manifestations of the star of Dawn and the Completion of Day is preserved in a very difficult text celebrating their birth in broad, bawdy burlesque, in which surprisingly El plays a coarse and somewhat ridiculous role. We have related this to the union of migrant graziers with the people of the land they grazed. It may reflect ties of intermarriage under the Semitic convention of *bîna* marriage, according to which a wife continues to live with her father's people and is visited only periodically by her husband, like Samson with his wife at Timnah (Judges 15.1).

THE AGRICULTURAL CYCLE

Since the myth of Baal in the Ras Shamra texts is intelligible only if related to the cycle of the agricultural year, we should study this cycle.

After the long drought of at least five summer months, relieved only by dew and local irrigation, the inhabitants feel a great tension and anxiety, increased by the autumn siroccos. In September the harvest, except the olives, is completed with the gathering of the grapes. Then the corn which has been threshed through late summer and other crops, such as dried figs, are brought in from the threshing-floors in winter storage. This is the Ingathering mentioned in the Old Testament, still a matter of some ceremony in the simpler Arab villages. From the Old Testament we see that it was an occasion of rejoicing.

This had the significance of a New Year festival in Israel also. It is significant that in an agricultural calendar from Gezer of about the tenth century B.C. the year begins with the Ingathering. That this should be associated with the new year rather than the end of the year is probably connected with the conception that the New Year ceremony with all its natural anxiety should begin auspiciously with the mood of thanksgiving and rejoicing in the spirit expressed in the Psalm,

Our God, our help in ages past,
Our hope for years to come.

The harvest rejoicing, however, only partially relieved the peasant's anxiety. The soil lay baked hard after the long summer drought, and could be ploughed for the new season's crop only after it had been softened by the first rains of winter. If these were long delayed, the growing season would be shortened and the corn might not come into ear before the onset of the siroccos of early summer finally checked the growth. In this case the crop would be nothing but straw, a disaster noticed by Amos (4.7):

And I also withheld the rain from you,
When there were yet three months to the harvest.

The tension was relieved by the rites of the great autumn festival. As in the spring New Year festival in Mesopotamia, the reality of the menace to order in nature was visualised and depicted as a 'showdown' between the forces of life, fertility and order in nature, and the forces that would destroy

them. Emotionally involved in the struggle, the people relieved their tension and purged their anxiety in their co-operation with the power of order. There is unfortunately practically no rubric to the Canaanite Baal myth to indicate an accompanying ritual, and it is not certain that there was a ritual conflict. The texts themselves, however, are sufficiently dramatic to evoke such a conflict even without visual aid.

The conflict was a prelude to Baal's victory as champion of the order decreed by the gods and vital to men and nature. This is the element of imitative magic, influencing Providence by auto-suggestion. It is an important element in the liturgy of festivals at vital seasonal crises, carrying with it all the intensity of the commitment of prayer. A striking example of imitative magic, the more so as it comes from a relatively sophisticated religion, was the Jewish rite of pouring water over the altar at the New Year Feast of Tabernacles, so that the people might enjoy the blessing of the rains in the new season, as an orthodox Rabbi explicitly states. We shall find striking correspondence between the ideology of the Canaanite and Hebrew New Year, especially in the important particular of the effective realisation of the power and authority of God as King, the vital issue also in the Babylonian New Year festival.

The identification of the powers of Chaos with water in the Baal myth of Ras Shamra and in Hebrew psalms relevant to the same occasion (e.g. Psalm 93) may seem at first sight odd in Canaan, where the great enemy was not water but drought. The motif may indicate the influence of the more sophisticated Mesopotamian New Year liturgy, but it may also have relevance to local conditions. The eroded hillsides of Syria and Palestine attest the menace of the torrential 'early rains' if they are uncontrolled. In the coastal plain by Ras Shamra, at present intersected by drainage channels, the heavy rains of early winter, if the natural watercourses were dammed back by heavy seas, might well destroy agricultural land and the crops sown there unless Providence intervened.

As a rite of imitative magic, the whole year's natural processes were visualised in the cycle of the Baal myths of Ras Shamra which depict the conflict of Baal with Mot (Sterility, Death), culminating in the ultimate victory of Baal. Here again the issue is the kingship, and in our citation of the text clear reference to the autumnal New Year will be noticed.

The cereal crops, barley and wheat in that order, are sown over a period of two months according to the old Gezer calendar, and if the season is favourable they come into ear in time to enjoy the benefit of the intermittent and lighter 'latter rains' at the end of spring in February or March. At this time natural growth is gathered from among the growing corn by the women as fodder for the domestic beasts, to which there is a reference in the legend of Prince Aqht, whose sister

Sweeps the dew off the barley.

That is to say, she is up early gathering fodder.

Canaan celebrated its agricultural festivals at the main seasonal crises of the beginning of the barley harvest, the end of the wheat harvest, conventionally fifty days or seven weeks later, and the Ingathering at the New Year season. The Canaanites observed a rite of desacralising the new crop, or releasing it from direct association with the forces of the supernatural for common use. Thus the first or last sheaf was beaten out and parched with fire, as in Israel (Leviticus 2.14). This was represented as the vengeance of Baal's sister Anat on Mot for the death of Baal at the time of the drought of summer.

In March vines are dressed on their terraces, and in the free period before harvest the peasants might move out to give their domestic animals the advantage of the spring growth in uncultivable regions at some distance from their home. The writer remembers a spring day spent with peasants from Beitin (Biblical Bethel) encamped for this spring grazing ten miles away in a wadi about five miles north of Jericho. Grazing rights of such migrants are often secured by intermarriage and we have related one of the mythological and ritual texts of Ras Shamra to such circumstances.

Opposite left: two silver figurines of Astarte indicated by her Hathor coiffure from the sanctuary at Nahariya on the coast of northern Palestine. c. 1500-1200.

Opposite right: stele depicting the fertility-goddess Ishtar of Arbela in her warlike character on her cult-animal the lion, from Tell Ahmar. c. eighth century B.C. Louvre.

Below: caryatid figurines of Astarte. Phoenician ivory from Nimrud, ninth century B.C.

The Myths

The tablets at Ras Shamra were discovered in a priest's house adjoining the temple of Baal. Their arrangement has been a problem to scholars, and their unity is also in question. Three fragments describe how Baal asserts his royal authority on behalf of the great gods against the arrogant waters Sea-and-Ocean Current. This is a Canaanite version of the theme we have met in the Babylonian New Year liturgy, in which Marduk asserts his royal authority against Tiamat. Other texts from the Baal cycle of myths describe the vicissitudes of Baal as the power manifest in the rains and thunderstorms of winter and in the vegetation which flourishes then, but wilts and dies in the summer heat, the season when Mot, Death or Sterility, prevails. Here the Baal myth has obvious affinities with the Tammuz mythology and hymns in Mesopotamia. Within the latter group of Baal texts there are references to themes which are not dealt with in the texts found so far. Thus in what we regard as the beginning of this text-complex, the goddess Anat, Baal's sister and vindicator, who is the protagonist at this stage, greets Baal's messengers, Vine and Field, with the questions:

What enemy rises up against Baal?
What foes against Him who Mounteth the Clouds?
Have I not smitten Sea, Beloved of El?
Have I not annihilated Ocean Current, the great god?
Have I not put a muzzle on Tannin?
Have I not smitten the Crooked Serpent,
The Close-coiling One with Seven Heads?
I have smitten the Darling of the deities of the underworld Mot,
Who strideth on with prodigious haste.
I have smitten the Bitch of the gods Fire,
I have annihilated the Daughter of El Flame.

The fact that these exploits are attributed to the goddess Anat as well as to Baal suggests that perhaps a substantial mythology from her shrine and cult is yet to be discovered, perhaps pertaining to summer festivals, when Baal was in eclipse. This, however, is but a conjecture, and since such liturgies were probably complementary to the Baal myth, probably nothing substantial has been lost, though the passage quoted above indicates that the texts are not complete.

THE BAAL MYTH

The three texts which culminate in the victory of Baal over Sea-and-Ocean Current and his establishment as King open with a description of the arrogance of 'Prince Sea, even Ocean Current the Ruler'. He intimidates the divine assembly under El, which abjectly acquiesces in his demand for tribute, including Baal as a slave. Baal is put on his mettle; he leaps up, seizing some weapon 'in his hand, a knife in his right hand', and is barely restrained from diplomatic outrage by the goddesses Anat and Athtarat (Astarte). Nevertheless he expels Sea's envoys with indignity, lashing their buttocks. Thus Baal emerges, like Enlil, as champion of the order of the divine court against the menace of chaos.

Baal is encouraged for the open conflict, which is now inevitable, by the divine craftsman, the Skilful and Percipient One, who at the outset of the text emphasises the issue, the kingship:

Have I not told thee, O Prince Baal,
Have I not repeated, O Thou who Mountest the Clouds?
Behold, thine enemy, O Baal,
Behold, thine enemy thou shalt smite,
Behold, thou shalt subdue thine adversaries;
Thou shalt take thine eternal kingdom,
Thy sovereignty everlasting.

Here it will be noted that the metric arrangement with its cumulative parallelism and even the language is repeated in Psalm 92:

For lo, thine enemies, O Lord,
For lo, thine enemies shall perish;
All evil-doers shall be scattered.

The divine craftsman furnishes Baal with a mace and, since he was also the master of incantation as well as an artisan, designates its purpose by its name, making it effective to that end:

The Skilful One hews out a double mace,
And proclaims its purpose,
'Thy name is Driver;
Driver, drive Sea,
Drive Sea from his throne,
Even Ocean Current from the seat of his sovereignty.
Thou shalt soar and swoop in the hand of Baal,
Even as an eagle in his fingers.
Strike the shoulders of Prince Sea,
Even the breast of Ocean Current the Ruler.'

Baal begins his onset, but in such a heroic conflict Sea is not immediately overcome:

Then soars and swoops the mace in the hand of Baal,
Even as an eagle in his fingers.
It smites the shoulders of Prince Sea,
Even the breast of Ocean Current the Ruler.
Sea is strong; he does not subside;
His strength is not impaired;
His dexterity fails not.

The attack is renewed with another mace Expeller, and described in epic repetition. This time Sea is struck 'between the eyes', which means also in Semitic languages 'between the wells', and is prostrated. The victory of the hero, as in the Gilgamesh epic in Israel and generally in Semitic convention, is celebrated by a female, the goddess Athtarat, who like the redoubtable Deborah of the Bible (Judges 5.28–30) exults over the defeated enemy:

Scatter him, O Mighty Baal,
Scatter him, O Thou who Mountest the Clouds,
For Prince Sea is our captive,
Yea, our captive is Ocean Current the Ruler.

The unruly waters are thus brought under control, distributed, so that they may be a benefit, and Sea is done to death.

At this significant part of the text, 'Let Baal reign!' is perhaps an interjection of the worshippers. It recalls the dramatic statement 'Yahweh has proved himself King!' in Psalms in the Old Testament. Many of the Psalms contain the same basic elements of decisive conflict with what menaces the

Order of God, and the establishment of His government, or ordered rule, Hebrew *mishpat*, which means more than 'judgment', the conventional translation of the English versions.

The text from this point is fragmentary, alluding to various parts of the body. It is uncertain whether these details correspond to creation from the dismembered body of Sea-and-Ocean Current, like creation from the body of Tiamat in the Babylonian New Year liturgy, or to Baal's investiture with 'the tablets of destiny' and other insignia of royalty, like Marduk in that myth.

This was the Canaanite declaration and renewal of faith in Providence. Its theme, the effective assertion of the power and authority of Baal as king 'in the beginning', is a fitting one for the great autumn festival on the eve of the new season of agriculture. Admittedly, there is nothing explicit in the three fragments cited to associate this myth with the New Year festival. But Hebrew psalms on the same theme have this association. The closest Mesopotamian analogy is related to the New Year festival in the spring; and in the myth of Baal's conflict with Mot, which continues the theme of the effective kingship of Baal, there is explicit reference to the seasonal crisis in autumn.

The festival was known in Palestine when the Israelites settled there, and the basic theme and often the imagery of psalms on the Kingship of God from the liturgy of the New Year festival indicate its influence. It was probably the Canaanite liturgy that introduced the conception of the King-ship of God to Israel, who did not at first think of God as a king. It must be emphasised, however, that Israel developed the Canaanite conception far beyond its limitations in the nature-cult. The Israelites applied the cosmic theme of the conflict of God with the powers of Chaos to their experience in history in situations which, unlike events in nature, did not recur, but introduced God in confrontation with His people in an ever-fresh situation. So the liturgy of the New Year festival celebrating God's establishment of His government, or order, against the menace of Chaos became an assurance for Israel in the present vicissitudes of history. It was also a hope for the future, when, beyond all the frustrating incidentals of history, God would consummate His purpose, the final establishment of His reign as King.

BAAL AND ANAT

In the texts relating strictly to agriculture in the forthcoming year, Baal is entertained at the direction of the goddess Anat, to symbolise his return and activity after his death and confinement in the underworld. The goddess proves her vitality by herding 'young men' into her temple and indulging in a blood-bath:

She prepares seats for the warriors,
Dressing tables for the soldiers,
Footstools for the heroes.
Violently she smites and gloats,
Anat cuts them down and gazes;
Her liver exults in mirth,
Her heart is filled with joy,
For in the hand of Anat is victory,
For she plunges her knees in the blood of the soldiers,
Her loins in the gore of the warriors
Till she has had her fill of slaughtering in the house,
Of cleaving among the tables.

The bloody work done, the redoubtable goddess cleanses and resanctifies the temple, and with truly divine aplomb turns to her own toilet:

She scoops up water and washes,
Even dew of heaven, the fatness of the earth,
The rain of Him who Mounts the Clouds,
The dew which the skies pour forth,
The rain which is poured forth by the stars;
She sprays herself with the perfumes of a thousand mountains,
Her slops in the sea (are cast).

It is difficult to explain this curious text. It may relate to an episode in the cycle of myths from the cult of Anat of which we have so far only fragments. In its full context its relevance would doubtless be clearer. But as an introduction to the Baal myth which follows, it is in our opinion related to the transitional period between the sterility of summer and the rains of the new season, which are mentioned in the sequel when the 'house of Baal' is completed. The extravagant blood-letting may relate to a rite of imitative magic to promote a liberal release of new life in the new season of agriculture, blood being to the ancient Semite the seat of life. The blood-letting of the 'prophets' of Baal in the invocation of rain during the famous ordeal with Elijah or Carmel (1 Kings 18. 44–45) may be such a rite.

The sequel, unfortunately fragmentary, alludes to a love-charm for Baal and his 'girls', probably partners in a sacred marriage in anticipation of fertility. These nymphs are suggestively named the Plump Damsel, which reflects the oriental taste in feminine beauty and alludes to the fattening of the land and its fattening produce, Dewy the Daughter of Showers and the Earth-Maiden the Daughter of the Wide World.

THE BUILDING OF THE HOUSE

Baal and Anat exchange messages which anticipate the favour of Anat as a fertility goddess and Baal's potency with his arms of thunder and lightning, the herald of the rain. The building of the 'house' of Baal is canvassed by Anat and is ultimately sanctioned by El and built by the Skilful and Percipient One. Here we note the characteristics of epic style in the repeated entreaty to have the 'house' built and the account of the building. The occasion to which the myth at this point was relevant is clearly stated. The completion of the house symbolises the summit of the power of Baal in the fertility cult, a king with a castle. This motif is found also in the Old Testament, e.g. Micah 4.1 and Isaiah 2.2, where the association significantly is with God's exaltation as King and the imposition of His order, or government. In the Canaanite myth the completion of the 'house' of Baal is anticipated as the occasion for Baal's manifestation in the storms of winter:

Moreover Baal will send abundance of his rain,
Abundance of his moisture with snow,
And he will utter his voice in the clouds,
He will send his flashing to the earth with lightning.

It may be that the 'tabernacles', or bivouacs of green branches, which were built in Israel at this seasonal festival, were, in the Canaanite prototype of the New Year festival, symbolical in some way of the building of the 'house' of Baal.

The culmination of the erection of the 'house' of Baal is the opening of a roof-shutter, on which attention is focused by the literary convention of an altercation between the divine craftsman, the Skilful and Percipient One,

Bronze figurine of the war-god Reshef from Megiddo, c. 1500-1200 B.C. Archaeological Museum, Jerusalem.

who urges its installation, and Baal, who will, ostensibly, have none of it. First, however, the 'house' is built:

They have gone to Lebanon with its trees,
To Shiryon with its choice cedars;
Fire is set in the mansion,
Flame in the palace;
Lo, a day, a second day;
The fire consumed in the mansion,
Flame in the palace,
A third, a fourth day,
Fire consumed in the mansion,
Flame in the palace,
A fifth, a sixth day,
Fire consumed in the mansion,
Flame in the palace,
Then on the seventh day
Fire went out in the mansion,
Flame in the palace,
Silver was melted into plates,
Gold into blocks,
Baal the Mighty exulted,
'I have built my house of silver,
My palace of gold'.

Then follows a hearty house-warming, which has its counterpart in Solomon's hecatombs of communion-offerings at the dedication of the Temple, which, significantly, fell at the same season in the month of Etanim ('the Regular Rains'), and indeed at the New Year festival:

Baal arranged the menage of his house,
Hadad arranged the menage of his palace.
He has slaughtered oxen and sheep,
He has felled bulls and fatlings,
Rams, yearling calves,

Now follows the significant installation of the roof-shutter, which has been emphasised by disputation. The relation of this to an all-important ritual of imitative magic is obvious from the sequel:

And cause the clouds to be opened with rain
When the Skilful One opens the window.

The roof-shutter is opened and rain and thunder ensue, such as are associated with late autumn in Syria, when the great New Year festival was observed.

A king with a castle at the height of his power, Baal thunders forth his challenge to all enemies:

O enemy of Hadad, how dismayed art thou
How dismayed at the weapon of our strength?
The eyes of Baal anticipate his hands,
When the cedar spear is brandished in his right hand.
Now that Baal returns to his house
Shall any, king or no king,
Make the earth his dominion?

Baal defies Mot (Death and Sterility) himself:

I shall indeed send a guide for the god Mot,
A herald for the Hero, beloved of El,
To call Mot to his grave,
To conceal that 'darling' in his tomb.
I alone am he who will reign over the gods,
Yea, be leader of gods and men,
Even marshal the multitudes of earth.

Stele dedicated by the Egyptian architect Amenemopet, shown with his son, to Mekal, possibly 'the Annihilator', the plague-god Reshef. The stele was at Bethshan, which is a notorious malarial region. The god's identity is indicated by his gazelle horns and his power of life as well as death is indicated by the *ankh* sign and *was* septre. *c.* 1300 B.C. Archaeological Museum, Jerusalem.

The underworld where Mot reigns is described in the account of Baal's embassy:

..., his city Ruin,
Dilapidation is the throne on which he sits,
Loathsomeness is the land of his inheritance.

In anticipation of the tension between fertility and sterility in the peasant's year, Mot returns a defiant answer:

Though thou didst smite Lotan the Primeval Serpent,
And didst annihilate the Crooked Serpent,
The Close-coiling One of Seven Heads,
The heavens will dry up, yea languish;
I shall pound thee, consume and eat thee,
Cleft, forspent and exhausted,
Lo, thou art gone down into the throat of the god Mot,
Into the gullet of the Hero, Beloved of El.

The reference to Baal's exploit against Lotan, the Crooked Serpent, the Close-coiling One of Seven Heads, is interesting, since it is retained as a tradition of the triumph of God's Order against Chaos in the cosmic conflict in the Old Testament. Isaiah 27.1 refers to God's decisive 'showdown' with 'Leviathan the Primeval Serpent, Leviathan the Crooked Serpent, the dragon that is in the sea'. Similarly in Job 26.13:

His hand pierced the Primeval Serpent.

BAAL'S DEATH AND DESCENT TO THE UNDERWORLD

Mot's vaunts are not in vain, since in another text Baal yields to his adversary and is eventually summoned to the underworld:

And thou, take thy clouds,
Thy wind, thy rain-clouds, thy rain,
With these thy seven lads,
Thine eight boar-hunters,
With thee the Plump Damsel, Daughter of Mist,
With thee Dewy, Daughter of Showers.
Thy face thou shalt surely set
Towards the Mountain of Concealment,
Take the mountain on thy hands,
The hill on the top of thy palms,
And descend to the House of Corruption in the underworld,
And thou shalt be numbered with those that go down into the earth,
Yea, thou shalt know annihilation as the dead.

Here Baal's 'boar-hunters' are probably a motif connected with the myth of Adonis ('the lord'), the Semitic fertility deity in the Greek version of the myth of the Syrian fertility-cult by Byblos, who was killed by a wild boar. This was possibly the origin of the ban on pork, later characteristic of the religion of Israel. In the description of the journey to the underworld, 'ars, which means both in Ugaritic and Hebrew also 'earth', the curious phrase 'take the mountain on thy hands' probably means simply 'grope thy way under', and the phrase 'be numbered with those that go down to the underworld' has its echo in Psalm 88.4, one of the many indications of the familiarity of Hebrew poets with the literature of ancient Canaan.

Before his descent to the underworld Baal mates with a heifer, presumably to provide for his survival in his cult-animal, a young bull, the birth of which is the subject of another text, which may be part of the cycle of the Baal myths. This incident may relate to the beginning of the breeding season, which on the modern Arab analogy would fall in April or May in order that

Phoenician ivory of head of female, possibly Ishtar, the so-called 'Mona Lisa' from Nimrud.

the calves should get the benefit of the spring pasture before the blasting siroccos of early summer.

The actual death of Baal and his descent to the underworld are not described, but they may well be visualised as occurring at the coming of the sirocco in early summer, before the annual vegetation wilts and the long summer drought sets in.

The text resumes after a considerable break with the lamentation and mourning rites of El for the dead Baal. The activity of the senior god, who is generally withdrawn in dignified remoteness, is probably the signal for the lamentation and mourning rites of the worshippers:

Verily Baal has fallen to the earth,
Dead is Baal the Mighty!
Perished is the Prince, lord of the earth!

Then the Kindly One, El the Merciful
Comes down from his throne, he sits on the footstool,
And (coming) off the footstool, he sits on the ground.
He lets down his turban in grief from his head;
On his head is the dust in which he wallows;
He tears asunder the knot on his girdle;
He makes the mountains re-echo with his lamentation,
And with his clamour the forest to resound.
Cheeks and chin he rends,
The humeral joint of his arm he scores,
The chest as a garden plot,
Even as a valley-bottom his back he lacerates.
He raises his voice and cries:
   Baal is dead! What is become of the Prince?
   The son of Dagan (is dead)! What of the multitudes (of men)?
   After Baal I shall go down to the underworld!

Here we have the mourning rites, familiar among the ancient Semites and in Israel. Generally at death, which is a crisis in society when the community is especially open to the influences of the supernatural, normal activities were suspended to thwart those forces. Thus the normal resorts were avoided, one forsook one's usual seat to sit on the ground, like Job on the village midden (Job 2.8), or begrimed the person or the clothes with dust and scored the face or the body. What was normally fastened one unfastened, a practice which is alluded to in Isaiah 58.6 as a fasting rite:

Is not this the fast I have chosen,
To loose the bands of wickedness?

The goddess Anat follows the lead of El in mourning, which is surely related to the mourning for Hadad-Rimmon, that is, Baal the Thunderer, in Zechariah 12.11, and specifically to the mourning of the women in Jerusalem for Tammuz which Ezekiel (8.14) deplores. This is certainly a summer rite, when Baal was at the nadir of his power. Similar rites are attested by Plato and by the mediaeval Arab writer Ibn an-Nadim, who describes a similar ritual mourning for Tammuz by the women of Harran in northern Mesopotamia. But this is obviously related to the offering of the last sheaf, which was probably later than Anat's mourning for Baal in the Ras Shamra texts. More particularly the mourning for Baal of Anat, whose stock epithet is 'the Virgin', while she

. . . ranges
Every mountain to the heart of the earth,
Every hill to the midst of the fields,

may be connected with the mourning rite of the virgins of Israel mentioned in Judges 11.37–40. This passage is explained somewhat artificially as the commemoration of the mourning of Jephthah's daughter, who went with her companions and 'bewailed her virginity upon the mountains'.

After mourning, Anat sets out to recover the body of Baal for burial, enlisting the aid of Shapash, the sun-goddess, whose help is invaluable, since, according to ancient belief, the sun on its journey passed nightly under the earth:

Anat, too, goes and ranges
Every mountain to the heart of the earth,
Every hill to the midst of the fields.
She comes to the pleasant land of the Back of Beyond,
The fair tracts of the Strand of Death;
She comes upon Baal fallen to the ground.
. . . .

When at length she was sated with weeping,
Drinking tears like wine,
Aloud she shouts to Shapash the Light of the Gods,
Lift upon me, I pray thee, Baal the Mighty.

This is connected with the familiar motif in the fertility cult in the Near East, the search for the dead god by the fertility-goddess, as in Ishtar's search for Tammuz, Demeter's search for Kore, Aphrodite's search for Adonis and the search of Isis for Osiris.

The end of the rites of suspension after the burial of Baal is marked by a funeral feast, which is noticed in Deuteronomy 26.14 as a rite to be avoided in Israel.

A substitute is sought for Baal in his eclipse, and Athtar the Luminous, originally the god manifest in the bright Venus star and secondarily associated with vegetation, is proposed since his brightness might be thought to qualify him for the place of Baal, whose potent advent is signalised in lightning. But the attempt is abortive:

Thereupon Athtar the Luminous
Goes up to the crags of Saphon;
He takes his seat on the throne of Baal the Mighty.
His feet do not reach the footstool,
His head does not reach the top thereof.
Then Athtar the Luminous declares,
'I may not be king on the crags of Saphon'.
Athtar the Luminous comes down,
Down from the throne of Baal the Mighty,
And he reigns in the ground, god of it all.

Eventually the goddess Anat, having unsuccessfully interceded with Mot for the restoration of Baal, loses her patience and resorts to the high hand:

She seizes the god Mot;
With a blade she cleaves him;
With a shovel she winnows him;
With fire she parches him;
With a millstone she grinds him;
In the field she scatters him;
His remains the birds eat,
The wild creatures consume his fragments,
Remains from remains are sundered.

This is a rite similar to the desacralisation of the corn crop described in Leviticus 2.14:

You shall offer for the cereal offering of your first-fruits
crushed new grain from fresh ears, parched with fire.

A closer parallel is the desacralisation rite among the Arab peasants at Harran mentioned by Ibn an-Nadim, where the women ceremonially wept for Tammuz, who had been 'slain by his lord' by having his bones ground with millstones and scattered to the winds. The dating of this rite in mediaeval Harran in the month of Tammuz (July) indicates its relation to the end of the harvest.

THE RETURN OF BAAL AND MOT'S DEATH

The year rolls on, and with the end of the wheat harvest in mid-summer and the vengeance of Anat on Mot, the revival of Baal is anticipated. Expectation is roused by a dream communicated by El, which is probably the signal for the acclamation of the worshippers:

For Baal the Mighty is alive,
For the Prince, Lord of the Earth, exists!

The phrase, 'the Prince exists' *('it zbl)* is the response to the question 'Where is Baal?' *('iy zbl)* which was probably the real form of the name of Ahab's Phoenician queen Jezebel. In its Hebrew form, with *zebel* ('dung') for *zebûl* ('Prince') the name is a malicious perversion by a Hebrew scribe. It was probably given because the queen was born or expected at the time of year when the revival of Baal was anticipated. It may even be that it reflects the conception of the king's potency in his capacity of channel of the blessings of Providence in nature. Similar is the role of certain Mesopotamian kings in the sacred marriage with the representative of the fertility goddess. The return of Baal and its consequences in nature are visualised:

The skies rain oil,
The wadis run with honey.

This suggests 'the land flowing with milk and honey' as the description of the Promised Land, or the vision of renewed prosperity in Joel 3.18:

And in that day
The mountains shall drip sweet wine,
And the hills shall flow with milk.

Mourning women on sarcophagus of King Ahiram of Byblos (twelfth century B.C.). They bare and lacerate their breasts and rend their dishevelled hair, the conventional mourning rites in the ancient Near East. National Museum, Beirut.

Eventually Baal returns, having first wrought vast desolation in the underworld and apparently dethroned Mot, a motif which recalls Nergal's treatment of the Queen of the Underworld, Ereshkigal, in a Mesopotamian text cited on page 23.

The dethronement of Mot, however, has only a seasonal significance. He again emerges 'in the seventh year' to challenge Baal in a critical conflict, which is one of the most graphic texts in the Baal myth. After defiance and recriminations against Baal:

They glare at each other like glowing coals;
Mot is strong, Baal is strong;
They thrust at each other like wild oxen;
Mot is strong, Baal is strong;
They bite like serpents;
Mot is strong, Baal is strong;
They kick like stallions;
Mot is down, Baal is down on top of him.

Logically we do not expect this scene after the description of Mot's death at the hands of Anat. But this is a pointed reminder that the texts, for all their literary form and finish, were not merely literary products, but developed from a primary association with ritual. In the last passage, 'the seventh year' may simply mean 'eventually' according to a well-known literary convention. But it may also refer to a septennial ritual, like the sabbatical year in Israel, when the land was allowed to lie fallow, an artificial famine observed in order that the powers of sterility might have free play and exhaust themselves so that the next period might be one of plenty. The passage in the Baal text may reflect a variant of this rite, whereby it was thought to exhaust the power of Mot and by Baal's victory predispose the issue for the future.

This then is the main tenor of the Canaanite myths of the fertility cult. As part of the liturgy of the fertility cult at significant crises in the agricultural year in Canaan, those myths became familiar to the Israelites. In their new lives as agriculturists, they adopted the seasonal festivals and, as is apparent from the denunciation of the prophets, much of the ritual and ideology of the Canaanite fertility cult in spite of official measures against such practices. Some elements of those seasonal festivals, however, were sublimated in the

Below: damascened bronze socketted axe from Ras Shamra (c. 1600 B.C.) cast with the forequarters of a boar. As indicated by the animal, which was considered unclean among the Semites, it was an import, probably from the kingdom of Mitanni in northern Mesopotamia. National Museum, Aleppo.

Opposite: capture of a wild bull, approached by the use of a decoy cow. Gold repoussé work from Vaphio, Greece, c. 1500 B.C. National Museum, Athens.

worship of Solomon's Temple, notably the conception of the Kingship of God won in conflict against the unruly waters and other forces of primaeval Chaos. This will be one of the major themes of our study of mythology in the Bible. The many echoes of the Canaanite myth of Baal in his conflict with Mot, on the other hand, are rather in the nature of imagery in the Prophets, Psalms and wisdom literature in the Old Testament.

THE MARRIAGE OF THE MOON-GOD AND MOON-GODDESS

An instance of the adaptation of a myth relating to deified forces of nature to a social occasion is possibly the myth of the marriage of the Moon-god (Yerah) with the Moon-goddess (Nikkal). This myth, being highly anthropomorphic, is valuable evidence for social usage, which may be paralleled in simple Arab peasant society at the present day.

First the proposal is made by a representative of the bridegroom, as among the Arabs, not to the bride herself, but to her father:

The Moon, the Luminary of Heaven, sends
To Hrhb, the Summer's King:
'Give Nikkal; the Moon will pay the bride-price;
Let 'ib ('the fruitful one') enter his house,
And I will give her bride-price to her father,
A thousand pieces of silver, yea ten thousand of gold;
I will send gems of lapis lazuli;
I will make her fallow land into a vineyard,
The fallow field of her love into orchards.

The bride's father, as among the Arabs, affects reluctance:
O gracious one among the gods,
Affiance thyself to Baal,
Wed the Plump Damsel, his daughter,
I will introduce thee to her father Baal.
Athtar is amenable in the matter of bride-price,
Go to *ybrdmy*,
The Lion will give the daughter of his father in exchange.

Here we regard 'the Lion' as Athtar the Venus star, the brightest luminary in those latitudes after the moon itself. This identification is suggested by the fact that the lion is the cult-animal of the fertility goddesses Ishtar in Mesopotamia and Anat in Canaan. Ishtar was derived from the astral god of the desert Athtar.

The Moon-god himself presses his suit:
Nay, but let Nikkal herself answer me,
Then afterwards make me thy son-in-law.

The bride-price is then paid, which is characteristically a transaction involving all the family:
The Moon paid the bride-price for Nikkal,
Her father set the beam of the balances,
Her mother set the pan of the balances,
Her brothers arranged the standard weights,
Her sisters the weights of the scales.

The second part of the text actually names the bride *Prbht*, and it is our opinion that the text of the divine marriage was recited as an auspicious incantation in an actual marriage. The reference to the Moon-goddess as 'the daughter of the Summer's King' may refer to the goddess manifest in the new moon after harvest. This is the favourite season for marriage among the Arabs of Syria and Palestine, because then they have the leisure and affluence required for the lavish entertainment of a wedding.

Two ivory panels from the royal couch in the palace of Ras Shamra (*c.* 1300 B.C.) The upper panel depicts the king's deeds in war and hunting and his queen. The panel is flanked by the fertility-symbol of the tree of life as a stylised palm with the Egyptian lotus flower. The lower panel depicts the royal pair after marriage. The heir-apparent is shown in the central panel, so designated, as in the legend of King Krt in the Ras Shamra texts, by being suckled by the goddess Anat. For the sake of symmetry in composition the figure of the prince is repeated. National Museum, Damascus.

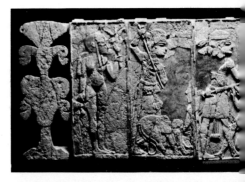

The King

Among the Ras Shamra tablets there are two texts of epic style and proportions about the ancient kings Krt and Dn'il.

THE LEGENDS OF KRT

The first is a legend which describes how Krt's numerous progeny was wiped out and he was left without a successor. Possibly in ritual incubation he receives revelation from El, who is interested in such public concerns and particularly in the king, who is described as 'the son of El' and the Servant of El, as David and his descendants were 'the Servant of God'. Directions are given for Krt to go wooing with a retinue of all his subjects, as an army, a reflection of the convention of marriage by force. This convention survives in the Arabic phrase for marriage, 'snatching the bride', and in the custom of the groom raising the bride's veil with the point of a sword. The reluctant father of the bride is eventually brought to acquiesce.

In epic convention this is narrated as it happened, practically verbatim, and so Krt won his bride. His wedding is blessed by divine guests and eight daughters are born. His eldest (Yasib, 'he who will succeed') is designated as heir, singled out as such by being described as suckled by the goddess Athirat and Anat, a motif which is depicted, perhaps as a charm, on a panel of the royal couch from the palace at Ras Shamra. By a special revelation, however, the eighth daughter is designated as of special significance. This may refer to eventual succession by another dynasty, the legitimacy of whose rule it was the object of the text to emphasise.

Meanwhile the king had failed to fulfil a vow to the goddess Athirat which he had made on his way to win his bride, and as a result becomes seriously ill. He is mourned by his youngest daughter 'Octavia' and a loyal son Ilha'u in what we shall notice as language which strongly expresses the 'divinity that doth hedge a king'. Nature itself languishes with the king's illness, and the heir-apparent attempts to persuade his father to abdicate, since during his illness justice is suspended. Here the lad may be quite genuinely alarmed at the evident curse on the king which his illness implied. Since the king as 'servant' or 'son' of God was the channel of divine blessings, the prince might well apprehend the serious consequences of the curse on nature and society. But his fears, or possibly his ambitions, are premature. By the favour of El, the king's sickness is exorcised by an image of clay and dung, and he revives to surprise his aspiring son by a good round oath:

May Horon break, O son,
May Horon break thy head,
Even Athtarat the Name-of-Baal thy pate!

THE LEGENDS OF KING DN'IL

The other text, entitled *'Aqht*, the name of the prince who is its hero, introduces King Dn'il, who has passed into Hebrew tradition as one proverbial for wisdom, righteousness and effective intercession (Ezekiel 14.14, 20). He is found in the sanctuary of El, clad in a loincloth, like young Samuel (1 Samuel 2.18), as one devoted temporarily to the shrine, probably for the purpose of securing an oracle in ritual incubation. This convention is paralleled in Solomon's dream at the sanctuary of Gideon (1 Kings 3.4–15) and among the Arabs, where dreams at a place associated with one regarded as an intercessor are accepted as revelations. The king makes food and drink offerings to the gods for six days,

Then on the seventh day
Baal profers his intercession
For the impotence of Dn'il the Dispenser of Fertility,
Even for the groaning of the hero, the man of Hrnm,
That he has no son like his brother,
Even a root like his kinsman.

The description of a desirable son and heir follows and, between the intercession of Baal and the birth of the son, is repeated four times. It was obviously meant to serve as a mirror of filial duties, and as a social ideal in ancient Canaan, it is worth quoting with comment. The heir of the king, as head of the community, must maintain the cult which gave the community cohesion. He is

One who may set up the stele of his ancestral god
In the sanctuary which enshrines his forefather,
Who may pour out his liquid-offering to the ground,
Wine to the dust after him.

Such a stele may be illustrated by the standing stones set up in a Canaanite sanctuary at Hazor in Palestine in the fourteenth century B.C. The ancestor, as the possessor of the blessing of the god or of his 'spirit', might be thought of as the extension of the presence and effective power of the god, and this may be the explanation of the description of dead kings of Ugarit as divine in a certain king-list from the palace. The ancestor thus commemorated by the pillar, and possibly buried under a cairn known in Hebrew as *bamah*, generally rendered in English versions as 'high place', would thus correspond to the *weli*, a person once noted as the recipient of the blessing of God, who

Below left: plan of a Canaanite temple (fourteenth century B.C.). The temple was tripartite with entrances on the same axis, as was Solomon's Temple.

Below right: the well of Jericho, the scene of Elisha's restoration of the water (2 Kings 2.19-22).

is treated among the Arabs as a patron saint. The blessing, which may be continued through continuance of divine grace shown to the ancestor, is the fruit of the field, which was peculiarly under the influence of the dead according to ancient belief. Installations of grave-apertures or hollow pipes communicating with the grave for the liquid offerings mentioned in the above text have been found at Ras Shamra and also at Samaria.

THE BIRTH OF AQHT

The son, like his father before him, must preserve the integrity of the community and its association with its gods by the communion-offering, where part of the victim is offered to the god and the rest eaten by the people. He is thus

One who may eat his slice in the temple of Baal,
His portion in the temple of El.

He must maintain his father's good name for the hospitality about which the Semitic community was reputedly punctilious. So an important duty was

Heaping up the platters of his company,
Driving away any who would molest his night-guest.

He must also safeguard his father's honour on any occasion when he was liable to expose himself when drunk. This might occur either in social conviviality or in the vintage at the Ingathering, in which it would have been regarded as ingratitude not to indulge. So another duty was

Holding his hand when he is drunk,
Carrying him when he is full of wine.

He must be diligent in his father's business,
Plastering his roof when it is muddy,

an allusion to the rolling of the flat oriental roof after rain to keep the mud surface intact. Here we may have a relic of a Canaanite proverb. Lastly he has the duty of

Washing his garment when it is dirty,

perhaps an allusion to services of an intimate nature which the son performs for his father, so that no other person may put an evil spell on the king.

El accedes to Baal's request on behalf of Dn'il and communicates his decision to the king. Dn'il invites into his palace the Kathirat, either nymphs or women skilled in incantation, to lend their influence in sympathetic magic or in incantation so that his union with his wife might produce an heir. The description of the actual birth and infancy of the lad is lost in a lucuna of two whole columns, and when the young prince Aqht, perhaps meaning 'He who prevails', is introduced, he is a grown youth.

The text describes how the craftsman-god, the Skilful and Percipient One, passes by with a stock of bows, probably intended for the gods. Being entertained by Dn'il, he gives one to the king, who presents it to Aqht, apparently with the injunction to be careful to sacrifice the first fruits of his hunting to a god.

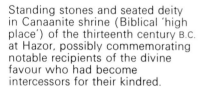

Standing stones and seated deity in Canaanite shrine (Biblical 'high place') of the thirteenth century B.C. at Hazor, possibly commemorating notable recipients of the divine favour who had become intercessors for their kindred.

THE DEATH OF AQHT

After a break the text describes the attempts of the goddess Anat to wheedle the bow from Aqht, whom she entertains at a party. This indicates probably that the bow had been intended for a god, perhaps herself. She offers first silver and gold for the bow:

Hear now, O hero Aqht,
Ask silver and I will give it thee,
Even gold and I will freely bestow it on thee,
But give me thy bow,
Let the Sister of the Prince take thine arrows.

But Aqht will not agree, and she next offers immortality:

Ask life, O hero Aqht,
Ask life and I will give it thee,
Immortality and I will freely grant it thee.
I will make thee number years with Baal,
Even with the sons of El wilt thou tell months.
As Baal, even as he lives and is feted,
Lives and is feted and they give him to drink,
Singing and chanting before him,

Singing of him, even the Gracious One,
Even so will I give thee life, O hero Aqht.

This, however, is beyond the lot of the ancient Semite, and the realistic reply of Aqht is:

Fabricate not, O Virgin;
To a hero thy lies are trash.
As for mortal man, what does he get as his latter end?
What does mortal man get as his inheritance?
Glaze will be poured out on my head,
Even plaster on my pate,
And the death of all men will I die,
Yea, I will surely die.

The goddess affects amusement, but she is mortally offended, and the myth pursues the theme of the fatal vengeance of the spurned goddess, which we have noticed in the death of Enkidu after Gilgamesh's repulse of the love of Ishtar. So Anat traduces Aqht to El and extorts his sanction to punish the prince. She apparently lures him to a hunting party at a place called Abiluma ('Flowing Waters'), where she has him struck down by Ytpn, a hired thug, disguised as a hunting falcon. Thus Aqht is killed, apparently contrary to the intention of the goddess, who had intended simply to wound him, and the bow is lost in the sea.

Obelisks in temple, possibly of Reshef, at Byblos, commemorating theophanies to individuals. Late Bronze age (c. 1500-1200 B.C.).

Golden bowl with hunting scene from Ras Shamra, (fourteenth century B.C.). Provincial Mycenaean work with Canaanite motifs, e.g. pomegranate buds and sacred tree in the inner panel. National Museum. Aleppo.

With consummate dramatic art and suspense the death of Aqht is divulged only gradually. First his sister, the Maiden, notices vultures hovering, the sure tokens of a dead body. This fear is confirmed by the wilting of vegetation, which is the consequence of the contamination of blood shed in violence, as in the murder of Abel (Genesis 4.11–12). The blood, moreover, is that of the heir of the king; hence, a grievous famine is the outcome. So in the Krt legend, nature and the crops evidently languished during the king's severe illness.

DN'IL AS DISPENSER OF FERTILITY

The sequel introduces the ancient king in his role as the medium of divine blessing in nature. This is, we think, the significance of Dn'il's title *mt rp'i*, 'the Healer or Dispenser of Fertility', *rp'i* being the participle of a verb known in Hebrew as meaning generally 'to heal', but specifically 'to give fertility', as in the spring of Jericho fertilised by Elisha (2 Kings 2.21). So Dn'il performs his sacral office, praying for rain and dew. His prayers, however, do not avail, for his first reaction had been to rend his robe, an inauspicious action which induces a mood of mourning and apparently intensifies the curse on nature after bloodshed. This must now run its course:

For seven years Baal is restrained,
Yea, eight He who Mounts the Clouds,
Without dew, without showers,
Without upsurging of the lower deep,
Without the drum-roll, the voice of Baal,
For the robe of Dn'il the Dispenser of Fertility is rent,
Even the mantle of the hero, the man of Hrnm.

The king, however, continues his functions as Dispenser of Fertility and endeavours to counteract the famine by rites on such plants as had survived:

Dn'il investigates; he goes round his parched land,
He sees a plant in the parched land,
A plant he sees in the scrub.
He embraces the plant and kisses it.
Ah me for the plant!
Would that the plant might flourish in the parched land,
That the herb might flourish in the scrub,
That the hand of the hero Aqht might gather thee in,
That it might put thee in the granary.

This is doubtless a rite of imitative magic designed to multiply the fertility of the surviving plants to transmit fertility to the next crop. The king evidently is unaware that it is Aqht who is dead. This might be intended as dramatic irony to heighten the pathos of the denouement. It may be, on the other hand, that the elderly Dn'il had apprehended the flight of vultures over the palace as an omen of his own death, and blessed the fields for what he thought was the last time. In this case the drought continuing after Dn'il's prayer for rain and dew may have suggested that his potency as Dispenser of Fertility had failed.

The sad news of Aqht's death is broken to Dn'il and his daughter the Maiden by two messengers, and the king sets out to avenge his son's death and recover the remains from the gizzards of the vultures, to bury them and so remove the drought and famine from the land. Accordingly, he breaks the wings of the vultures, either by a missile or by a curse. Thus bringing them down one by one, he opens their gizzards. Failing to recover his son's remains, he restores the birds, until eventually he brings down *Sml*, the mother of the vultures:

Baal breaks the wing of *Sml*,
Yea Baal breaks her pinion,
She falls at his feet;
He splits open her inwards and looks.
There is fat, there is bone.
Thereupon he takes Aqht,
Emptying him from the vulture; he weeps and buries him,
He buries him in the darkness in concealment.

Horned incense altar from Megiddo (Late Bronze age, *c.* 1500-1200 B.C.). Archaeological Museum, Jerusalem.

Pottery incense burner from Canaanite temple at Bethshan with superimposed motif of serpent, as symbol of life and renewal. Thirteenth century B.C. Archaeological Museum, Jerusalem.

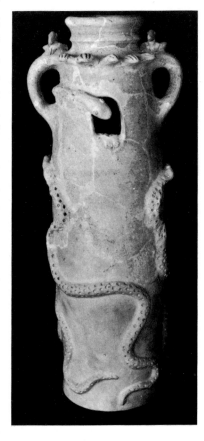

A connection between the death of Aqht and that of Mot at the hands of Anat, which clearly relates to the harvest rite of the desacralisation of the last sheaf (see page 87), has been suggested, but we consider the correspondence more apparent than real. There is, nevertheless, possibly some fusion of motifs between the harvest rite and a historical situation which has become the subject of legend. A rough analogy of this process is the Biblical tradition of the death of the seven sons of Saul in 2 Samuel 19.9–10. This is also associated with harvest rites and with birds of prey, which were expected to eat their bodies, but were prevented by the loyal act of Saul's concubine. This is certainly a case where local tradition of a harvest rite involving a human victim has either been fused with a historical situation or, as A. S. Kapelrud has proposed, has been utilised to sanction a political expedient. Whatever the historical situation in the Aqht legend may have been, it is quite obscured in the myth by the theme of a mortal's affront to the fertility goddess and her vengeance in the death of the hero, followed by drought and famine. At this point the Canaanite myth is evidently influenced by that part of the Gilgamesh epic dealing with Gilgamesh's repulse of Ishtar and her vengeance in the drought and in the death of Enkidu.

As in ancient Israel (Deuteronomy 21.1–9) in homicide cases, where the killer is unknown, a curse is pronounced upon the settlements nearest to the scene of the crime:

The King curses the Source of Water:
'Out upon thee, O Source of Water,
For upon thee lies the guilt of the slaughter of Aqht the hero,
Seek perpetual sanctuary,
A fugitive now and forever,
Now and for every generation!'
So says he, the staff in his hand signifying finality.

So Dn'il's curse runs upon two other localities which might have been responsible for the murder. Here the text gives an interesting insight into social convention, and the sequel, too, is of interest in illustrating mourning conventions, with professional mourners as in Ecclesiastes 12.5:

Dn'il reaches his house,
Dn'il lights down at his palace.
He has caused weeping women to enter his palace,
Even mourning women his court,
. . . .
They weep for Aqht the hero,
They shed tears for the offspring of Dn'il the Dispenser of Fertility;
From days to months,
From months to years,
Until seven years
They weep for Dn'il the hero,
They shed tears for the offspring of Dn'il the Dispenser of Fertility.

With this seven-year period of mourning we pass from legend to myth. It clearly refers to a seven-year famine, during which mourning is the appropriate mood. The seven-year famine is a motif where myth, or at least the stylistic character of myth, influences historical narrative, as in the Joseph story in Genesis. It is important to recognise this feature in order to delimit the strictly historical substance where it is coloured by mythology and folk-lore, as is inevitable where history is transmitted through oral tradition.

Above: coin of the Seleucid king Antiochus IV (175-164 B.C.) 'the god manifest' (*theos epiphanes*), with Zeus enthroned on the reverse, characterised by his thunderbolt, which suggests a natural assimilation to the native Baal-Hadad.

Below: relief in Assyrian style (late eighth century B.C.) of the Aramaean king Bar Rakkab, from Zenjirli near Aleppo. The flourishing plant in his hand symbolises life and health. Note the bull's head on his throne, the bull being the cult-animal of Baal-Hadad, the Divine King, whose executive the king was. This relationship is indicated by the name, or title, Bar-Hadad ('the son of Hadad'), borne by several kings of Damascus. The element Rakkab in the king's name may indicate 'charioteer', the stock epithet of Baal in the Ras Shamra texts being 'He who Mounts the Clouds' (rkb 'rpt).

THE MAIDEN AVENGES AQHT'S DEATH

The death of Aqht is avenged by his sister the Maiden, suggesting the role of the goddess Anat in the Baal myth. The unwonted role of the female suggests the suspension of normal activity in what the anthropologist van Gennep calls *saisons de passage*, phases of transition; here again indicating the intrusion of the myth of the nature cult into a historical or social legend. The Maiden, having girded herself with a sword and/or dagger, puts on cosmetics and a woman's robe, and at dusk is taken for Anat and admitted into the camp of Ytpn. She evidently suspects him as the henchman of Anat who has slain her brother. She is entertained in the camp. Ytpn boasts of his slaughter of Aqht, and pledges his further service. Her suspicions confirmed, the Maiden plies the thug with wine. Her purpose is probably to drug him and assassinate him. Here the text breaks off, and the rest may only be imagined. Three other fragments, however, continue the theme of the king Dn'il as the medium of fertility, and evidently the birth of another family was celebrated.

Thus, the ideal of the king in ancient Canaan is as the channel of divine blessing in nature. He is also the recipient of revelation, as Krt, and probably also Dn'il, in ritual incubation. He is also priest and personally performs sacrifice on behalf of the community. He is the Servant, the representative of the community in its 'service', or worship, of the gods. He is the executive of El, a relationship which is also expressed by the status of the king as 'son of El', the King paramount, whose province was particularly social relations. Thus, the king is the upholder of social justice. Dn'il's daily routine is described as follows:

He rises to sit at the entrance of the gate
In the place of the notables who are in the public place;
He decides the case of the widow,
He judges the suit of the orphan.

This is also the function of the king in the Krt legend, and his alleged failure is the basis of the demand for his abdication.

The peculiar status of the king as the representative of the community before God and the executive of God in society confers a blessing also on his family. Thus, the heir apparent of Krt is described as one.

Who sucks the milk of Athirat,
Who sucks the breasts of the Virgin (Anat).

This motif has been noticed in ivory sculpture from the palace of Ugarit, which recalls the Egyptian sculpture of the young Seti so nourished at the breast of a goddess.

SACRAL KINGSHIP

The conception of the king as the 'son of El' and as executive of God might, of course, lead to extravagant claims for the divine, as apart from the strictly sacral, status of the king. This is quite apparent in the mourning for the sick Krt:

How say they Krt is the son of El,
The offspring of the Kindly One and the Holy?
Or do gods die,
The offspring of the Kindly One not live?

This passage, however, should not be unduly pressed in the interests of the theory of divine kingship among the Canaanites, since its expressions were

induced by the emotional strain of lamentation. Nevertheless, the tradition of kingship was the ready tool of political propaganda as in the case of the successors of Alexander the Great in Syria and Mesopotamia, among whom Antiochus IV (175–164 B.C.) styled himself the God Manifest *(Theos Epiphanes)*. Thus applied, it was the object of prophetic criticism, as in Ezekiel's denunciation of the King of Tyre in the beginning of the sixth century B.C.

The situation of Tyre on its strong island fortress suggested to Ezekiel the Canaanite location of the seat of El. This was stated in the Ras Shamra texts to be:

At the well-head of the two streams,
In the midst of the source of the two deeps.

The reference to Dan'el, as he was spelt in the Ras Shamra Legend of Aqht, indicates Ezekiel's familiarity with the literary tradition of Canaan. In his reference to the confident assertion of the King of Tyre,

I sit in the seat of God
In the heart of the seas,

the prophet may well be alluding to the ancient myth, though the word he uses is the generic 'God' and not the proper name El, whom orthodoxy forbade him to recognise. In the same passage (Ezekiel 28.2–10) the repeated allusion to the king's 'wisdom', here the *savoir faire* of the man of the world, is probably an allusion to wisdom as the prerogative of El in Canaanite mythology, where he is respectfully addressed with the words,

Thy word, O El, is wise,
Thou art eternally wise.

So the king is pointedly reminded that he is not El, or God, but man – and like man shall be chastised.

In a sustained dirge Ezekiel (28.12–19) continues to lament the downfall of the King of Tyre from the uniquely exalted place of the king as reflecting the authority of God, the Divine King, and as admitted to sit enthroned, like the king of the House of David, at God's right hand (Psalms 80.17; 110.1).

In the first strophe of this passage (vv. 12–13), which has apparently suffered later expansion resulting in mixed imagery, Ezekiel probably originally depicted the King of Tyre as God's perfect seal, the medium of the divine authority. The king had the imprint of God's purpose for and through man distinctly set on him as the design and legend of the seal, thus reflecting the king as the representative of man created in the image of God. In the second strophe (vv. 14–15), which has also suffered elaboration by later hands, the king is depicted as established by the throne of God, the Divine King, flanked, like thrones in the ancient Near East, by winged sphinxes, the cherubs of the Old Testament, which were regarded as the guardians of the throne.

Thus established like the kings of the Davidic House enthroned by the right hand of God, the King of Tyre is depicted as 'consecrated on the mountain of God'. The prophet visualises the king as the representative of the Divine King, Baal in this case, on the holy mountain, or more particularly, as we know from the Ras Shamra texts, Mount Saphon, the seat of Baal. Here he walks amidst 'stones of fire', which may refer to the palace of Baal, the Divine King. This palace is depicted in the Ras Shamra texts as being built of various kinds of precious stones and gold and silver. The materials were fused with fire, which is said to have burned seven days in the 'house'. With the expulsion of the king by 'the protecting cherub' in the following strophe and his utter discomfiture before his fellow-kings in the rest of the passage, however, the prophet obviously uses the motif of the expulsion of Man (*'adam*) from the Garden of Eden, where the cherubim were appointed to exclude Man from Paradise.

The remarkable fact is that the essential elements of this ideology of kingship characterised the conception of kingship under the Davidic Dynasty in Jerusalem, and were developed in the eschatological conception of the Messiah. The study of the degree to which the royal ideology was assimilated under the House of David and in later Judaism and the early Christian Church and the degree to which it was modified, will be the subject of the final section of this book.

Opposite above left: ivory cover of cosmetic spoon from Lachish incised with stylised motif of the Tree of Life (Late Bronze age, *c.* 1500-1200 B.C.) Archaeological Museum, Jerusalem.

Opposite below: ivory plaque from the palace at Megiddo (*c.* 1350-1150 B.C.) incised with stylised motif of Tree of Life. Archaeological Museum, Jerusalem.

Opposite above right: offering to the dead king Ahiram of Byblos (twelfth century B.C.) seated on a throne flanked by two winged sphinxes. Compare the two winged 'cherubs' which flanked the ark in Solomon's Temple. The drooping lotus in the hand of the king indicates that he was dead. From his sarcophagus. National Museum, Beirut.

Above: ivory open-work carving depicting winged sphinxes, guardians of the Tree of Life, here stylised. The ram's head is an Egyptian motif, as often in such Phoenician sculptures, found in the Assyrian palace at Arslan Tash in northern Syria. It was part of the plunder from the palace of Hazael at Damascus. National Museum, Aleppo.

ISRAEL

Myth and History in the Old Testament

The first tangible ancestors of Israel were associated with northern Mesopotamia, the kindred of Abraham being mostly identified with settlements of Aramaean groups there into which Isaac and Jacob intermarried. Distinctive legal conventions in patriarchal tradition show the same affinity. Through such nomads Mesopotamian traditions were introduced to Palestine. Tales were told of the stupendous ziggurats, or staged temple-towers, which seemed to the nomad symbolic of the townsman's presumption, and their ruin seemed evidence of the wrath of God. Such was the origin of the story of the Tower of Babel (Genesis 11.1–9), to which is added the naive explanation of the diversity of races and languages by popular, and quite unscientific, etymology, which associated Babel (actually *bab-ili*, 'the Gate of God') with the Hebrew verb *balal* ('to mix up'). The Flood tradition in the Gilgamesh Legend, which retains most of its Mesopotamian features in Genesis ch. 6–8, also made a striking impression, and was widely known through the Near East, as is indicated by a fragment from about 1200 B.C. found at Megiddo in Palestine.

The tradition of archetypal man *('adam)* in the Garden of Eden with its tree of life, which really belonged to the royal ideology of Mesopotamia, was also transmitted and taken literally. Man's expulsion from the Garden possibly reflected the nomad's sense of deprivation, constantly being driven with his flocks from the cultivable land. The antipathy between agricultural settlers and nomad shepherds, which we have found already (see page 15) as the theme of a Sumerian myth explaining social conditions, is also reflected in the first part of the story of Cain and Abel (Genesis 4.1–8). The second part of the story of Cain (Genesis 4.9 ff) is, like the account of the name Babel, an aetiological, or explanatory, myth. It accounts for the wide-wandering habits of castes of nomad smiths (Hebrew *qayin* means 'smith') with their traditional skills, metallurgy and music (Genesis 4.21–22), and their safe-conduct in the places where they sojourned (Genesis 4.15). The mark of Cain was probably a tattoo mark, which often in the ancient Near East signified one's religion. Those nomad smiths, known in the Old Testament as Kenites, with whom the Hebrew intermarried, helped to transmit Mesopotamian traditions to Palestine, particularly the myths of origins and social relationships. These are incorporated in the first great narrative source of the Pentateuch in Genesis ch. 1–11, dating from the tenth century B.C., when they were made the vehicle of theology.

THE GREAT DELIVERANCE AND COVENANT

'Israel' denotes the sacral confederacy which originated in the deliverance of a number of displaced people, *khabiru* (hence 'Hebrews'), from state servitude in Egypt, and in the experience of adoption as a religious community under Divine Covenant at a holy mountain in the desert under the guidance of a great religious leader, Moses. The group who actually experienced the Great Deliverance and Covenant attracted others of their kindred in Palestine. The solidarity of the sacral community was effected and fostered by the re-enactment of the Great Deliverance and the Covenant in a sacramental experience analogous to the experience by which the Christian Church sustains its contact with its creative origin in the sacrament of the Lord's Supper. Through the dramatic enactment on regular religious occasions at the central sanctuary, the historical circumstances of the escape from Egypt and the Covenant were transformed. The recovery of the actual historical tradition is a critical exercise which is outside the scope of this book. In view of the importance of this tradition in Israel, however, and of the importance of distinguishing between myth and history, which are so often associated in the story of early Israel, we may venture some remarks on this subject.

In order that the experience of the Great Deliverance and the Covenant might be appropriated by those who had not actually participated and after the actual events had become more remote, they became more highly dramatised in vivid narrative, circumstantial detail and possibly also ritual. As a result, the tradition of the genesis of Israel, whatever its original historical character, has become a Drama of Salvation. This dramatical and theological character of the tradition transforms history, and incidentally renders in vain all attempts to reconstruct the circumstances of the Exodus by the literalistic interpretation of details. The first main narrative source from the tenth century B.C., known in Old Testament criticism as J, can be segregated by critical methods. Its source in a cult-drama then clearly emerges. It portrays an intensifying conflict between God and His people under their leader Moses and the forces which would frustrate them, under the Pharaoh. In the personal conflict between Moses and Pharaoh the latter, by a series of plagues to the disadvantage of the Egyptians, from which, unnaturally, their Hebrew servants and neighbours are exempt, is gradually compelled to let the Hebrews go. The drama is heightened by the intensification of the

Previous page: Cave 4 at Qumran near the monastery of the Sect of the New Covenant in the wilderness of Judah, about nine miles south of Jericho. In this cave many of the most valuable manuscript discoveries were made.

The ziggurat of Nanna the moon-god of Ur built by Ur-nammu (2250-2233 B.C.). It is one of the staged temple-towers which suggested to the nomad fathers of Israel the story of the Tower of Babel. Opposite is shown the south-western side; below is the north-eastern facade.

Copper-bearing mountains north of the Gulf of Aquaba, with mines from Solomon's time and before, worked by the Biblical Kenites.

plagues until the fatal plague in which the first-born of every Egyptian household, 'from the first-born of Pharaoh who sat on his throne to the first-born of the captive who was in the dungeon, and all the first-born of the cattle' (Exodus 12.29), is slain. At this point the Passover, a rite associated with the seasonal migrations of nomad shepherds originally independent of the Exodus, is utilised as ritual to heighten the drama, which culminates in the destruction of the Pharaoh and his army in the critical jeopardy of the Hebrews at the Sea of Papyrus Reeds (Exodus 14):

10. When the Pharaoh drew near, the people of Israel lifted up their eyes, and behold, the Egyptians were marching after them; and they were in great fear. And the people of Israel cried out to the Lord; 11. And they said to Moses, "Is it because there are no graves in Egypt that you have taken us away to die in the wilderness? What have you done to us, in bringing us out of Egypt?

12. Is it not this that we said to you in Egypt, 'Let us alone and let us serve the Egyptians?' For it would have been better for us to serve the Egyptians than to die in the wilderness."

13. And Moses said to the people, "Fear not, stand firm and see the salvation of the Lord, which He will work for you today; for the Egyptians whom you see today, you shall never see again.

14. The Lord will fight for you and you have only to be still. . . .

19b. And the pillar of cloud moved from before them and stood behind them.

20b. And there was the cloud and the darkness; and the night passed without the one coming near the other all night; 21b And the Lord drove the sea back by a strong sirocco all night, and made the sea dry land; (22. And the people of Israel went into the midst of the sea on dry ground . . . 23. The Egyptians pursued and went in after them . . .)

24. And in the morning watch, the Lord in the pillar of fire and of cloud looked down upon the host of the Egyptians, and discomfited the host of the Egyptians;

25. And the Egyptians said, "Let us flee from before Israel; for the Lord fights for them against the Egyptians."

27c. And the Lord routed the Egyptians in the midst of the sea; 28b. Not so much as one of them remained.

The recital of the Drama of Salvation culminated in a hymn of praise (Exodus 15.1–12, later expanded in vv. 13–18).

In the Drama of Salvation the emphasis is laid strongly on the immediate activity of God, whose saving power the worshippers acknowledged by emphasising the miraculous. Thus, for instance, the infection of all the waters of Egypt, the general infestation of frogs, hail and lightning and locusts do not affect the Hebrews. The nature of the narrative is coloured both by the cult-drama and by popular saga, as is clearly indicated by the statement that when the flies were removed not one remained, not one beast of the Hebrews died in the cattle-plague, and when the locusts were removed 'not a single locust was left in all the land of Egypt.'

THE ESCAPE AT THE SEA OF REEDS

The feature that arrests most readers in the Exodus story is the miracle of the Great Deliverance at the Sea, or Lake, of Papyrus Reeds, the water standing like a wall on each side of the path of the Hebrews (Exodus 14.22). When we sort out the various strands of the composite narrative, however, as we have just done in segregating the earliest source, we find that v. 22 is from the latest strand (fifth century B.C.), and that the earliest account is much more sober. It describes what might be no more than a sudden, and in those regions unusual, rain-storm. The storm converted a valley with ample ground-water, or the shallow end of a papyrus-fringed lake, after it had been parched by a sirocco, into a swamp which bogged down the pursuing Egyptians, so that the Hebrews escaped. In the hymn which was the culmination of the sacramental celebration of this Great Deliverance, we find that the psalmist has used his poetic licence to declare:

At the blast of thy nostrils the waters piled up,
The floods stood up in a heap. (Exodus 15.8)

This is the tradition which was eventually incorporated in the last prose version from the fifth century B.C., which is drawn up in Exodus 14.22. Here incidentally we may state that we do not deny divine intervention in the Great Deliverance. That, however, consisted not in the opening of the sea, but in the sudden unusual rain-storm at a place and time where it suited the purpose of God. The miracle lay not in a contravention of nature as Exodus 14.22 suggests, but in the coincidence. We may further add that the first step in the study of miracles in the Bible must not be from the point of view of theology or metaphysics, but from literary criticism in determining the chronological development of a tradition and the literary character of the sources in which it is attested.

THE APPEARANCE OF GOD AT SINAI

The Sinai theophany also in the context of the Covenant sacrament is similarly elaborated in cult-drama. Here an interesting feature is smoke and earthquake as concomitants of the appearance of God at Sinai (Exodus 19.16–18). The curious fact is that, whether the holy mountain is located in the south of the Sinai peninsula, the traditional location, or near the oasis of Kadesh in the north of the peninsula, which we consider the probable site, there has been no volcanic activity in the historical period. The nearest volcanic field in fact is in the northern Hejaz in the land anciently called Midian. Now in the tradition of Israel's Covenant experience mediated by Moses, there is a significant connection between Moses and the nomad tribe

Clay figurine from Saqqara near the pyramids of Gizeh in Egypt (c.1800 B.C.), inscribed with a curse and ceremonially buried. The deposit includes figurines of Amorite chiefs of Palestine and southern Syria roughly contemporary with Abraham.

of Jethro (Exodus 18), whose daughter he married (Exodus 2.16 ff). This was evidently a Kenite clan of nomad smiths, and was associated with Midian (Exodus 2.16 ff). When Moses joined them in 'the land of Midian' they may have wandered between the oasis of Kadesh and the depression north of the Gulf of Aqaba, where copper was mined in the escarpments east and west of the valley (later King Solomon's mines).

We suggest that when the Kenites, or Midianites, occupied the Kadesh oasis from their ancestral home in Midian in the volcanic mountains of the Hejaz, they brought with them the tradition and cult-legend of an original mountain-sanctuary, which now became attached to their new holy mountain in north Sinai, the scene of the Covenant mediated to Israel by Moses. The transference of a cult-legend and actually the name of the seat of the god to whom it originally pertained is indicated in the liturgy of the Canaanite New Year festival adapted in Israel to Mount Zion in Jerusalem. Mount Zion was said to be 'in the heights of Saphon' (Authorised Version 'on the sides of the North', Psalms 48.2), the seat of Baal in the Ras Shamra texts, known to be the conspicuous mountain Jebel al-Aqra in north Syria. Thus, fire, smoke and earthquake, volcanic phenomena, became the traditional signs of the advent of Israel's Covenanted God, as for instance in Isaiah's vision of his call (Isaiah 6). We take this to be in the Temple on the occasion of the autumn festival at the New Year season, when the victorious conflict of God with the powers of Chaos was celebrated, resulting in the establishment of His rule as King. It was also the occasion of the sacrament of the Covenant in the Temple in Jerusalem. This association would explain the bizarre imagery of God as 'the ancient of days' on His throne of fiery flames with wheels of burning fire in Daniel 7.9.

Throughout the books of Joshua, Judges, Samuel and Kings, our main sources for the history of Israel from about 1225 B.C. to the collapse of Judah in 586 B.C., the strictest literary criticism is necessary to distinguish sober history from history coloured by dramatic sacramental experience. Typical examples are the account of Joshua's conquests in Joshua 2−11 and oral saga with its schematising tendency, as in the tribal traditions in Judges, much of the tradition of Elijah and Elisha, and even occasionally the presentation of political history in Kings.

THE CONQUESTS OF JOSHUA

The account of the Israelite occupation of Palestine in Joshua 2−11 is based largely on the theme of the occupation of the Promised Land. It was celebrated in dramatic narrative and hymns of praise at the central sanctuary of the sacral confederacy in the days of the judges at Gilgal near Jericho. This is the 'myth', the oral element in the cult, behind which one must recover the historical nucleus of fact. The elaborated historical nucleus here is further elaborated by aetiological, or explanatory, myths, which grew up to explain for the satisfaction of pilgrims certain local features and place-names. For example, a prominent tree and stone-heap at the ruined city of Ai on one of the main roads taken by the pilgrims to the shrine of Gilgal were explained to the faithful as the places where the defeated king of Ai was respectively hanged and buried (Joshua 8.29). The Valley of Achor ('Troubling') south-west of Gilgal and Jericho, and the cairn of Achan (Joshua 7.26) are similarly explained.

Left: the land of Midian in the northern Hejaz across the Gulf of Aquaba, the original home of the Biblical Kenites and the region of their original holy mountain.

Below: mural painting from the tomb of Rekhmire (fifteenth century B.C.) near Thebes in Upper Egypt. It depicts displaced persons (*khabiru*, Egyptian *'apirw*, hence Hebrews) as state slaves moulding bricks for public works. It was from this class that Moses led a group out of Egypt, which became 'Israel' after the Covenant experience at the holy mountain in Sinai.

Left: in this photograph can be seen one of the natural pinnacles of rocksalt by the western shore of the Dead Sea, which suggested the tradition of Lot's wife.

Below: a nomad herdsman in the land of Moab, the last stage of the wandering of the Israelites before the main penetration of Palestine by way of Jericho.

A case similar to that of the Great Deliverance at the Sea of Reeds in Exodus 14 is that of the tradition of the preternaturally long day granted to Joshua to take full vengeance on the Amorites (Joshua 10.12–14). The earliest source here is the citation from the national epic 'the Book of Yashar':

'Sun stand thou still at Gibeon,
And thou, moon, in the valley of Aijalon.'
And the sun stood still and the moon stayed
Until the people took vengeance on their enemies.

There is nothing here that need refer to more than an atmospheric obscuration prolonging the darkness, which Joshua exploited to surprise his enemies, having advanced by a night march from Gilgal by Jericho. This is the historical nucleus. A later prose paraphrase in Joshua 10.13b, however, misunderstands the poetic citation and states:

The sun stayed in the midst of the sky,
And did not hasten to go down for about a whole day.

A preternatural miracle is thus made of the incident, an easy development, since in the earlier source too the natural phenomenon was ascribed to the immediate activity of God.

AETIOLOGICAL MYTHS

Aetiological myth amplifies historical tradition in the Pentateuch and in the historical books at many points. In the limited scope of this book, a few examples must suffice. The aetiological myth may be a narrative digression to explain a certain situation. Thus the ethnic affinity and political hostility of Israel and Edom are explained by the struggle of the twins Jacob and Esau in Rebekah's womb (Genesis 25.22). Israelite antipathy for her hostile neighbours Moab and Ammon is reflected in the libellous story of the origin of the two peoples from the incestuous union of Lot with his two daughters, Moab being explained as 'from my father' (Hebrew *me'abî*) and Ammon as 'the son of my kinsman' (Hebrew *ben-'ammî*). Local features and place-names are similarly explained. There is such a digression in the incident at the River Jabboq (Hebrew *yabboq*) where Jacob (Hebrew *ya'aqob*) wrestled (Hebrew *ye'abeq*) with the angel of God (Genesis 32.24) at Peniel ('the face of God'), explained as the place where Jacob saw the face of God (Genesis 32.30). This story serves also to explain the ritual taboo on the sinew of the hip for food by the story of God's dislocation of Jacob's thigh. This is also the object of the aetiological myth of the ark in the temple of Dagon at Ashdod (1 Samuel 5.1–5), to explain the ritual leaping over the threshold of the temple. Or again a prominent local feature might be so explained, as for instance the isolated salt-pinnacle south-west of the Dead Sea as the remains of Lot's wife (Genesis 12.26). The Gates of Gaza, the head of the wadi leading from north-west of Hebron to the coast of Askalon and Gaza were explained by the legend of Samson's exploit in carrying off the gates of Gaza and depositing them near Hebron forty miles distant! These are but a few instances of aetiological myth in the Old Testament, which must be critically segregated before a historical appraisal can be made.

THE STORIES OF SAMSON

The Samson cycle in Judges is particularly interesting. It is a hero-legend which has attracted to itself through local association aetiological legends explaining the origin of the rock-altar at Zorah (Judges 13.9 ff.) and local place-names such as Ramath-lehi, explained as the scene of Samson's exploit with the jaw-bone *(lehî)* of an ass (Judges 15.9–17), and the Partridge (literally 'Caller') Spring (Judges 15.18–20). Samson's destruction of the Philistines' corn by torches fixed to the tails of foxes may reflect a local ritual against mildew in the crops (Judges 15.4–5). The Latin poet Ovid mentions a similar rite for this purpose in April, when foxes with lighted torches attached to their tails were hunted about the Circus in Rome.

It is difficult not to associate the hero-legend of Samson (Hebrew *shimshôn*) with the cult-legend of Bethshemesh ('the shrine of the Sun'), which was only two and a half miles from Samson's reputed home at Zorah. Samson, who has been in his prime vigour in the summer, ends his days in darkness, which suggests winter. He grinds, repeating the weary round under external compulsion in the darkness of the prison.

Features in the Samson cycle which are common to the Greek myth of Herakles have also been noted: for example, the killing of a lion with his bare hands, betrayal by a woman, and the hero deciding his own death with the descent to the darkness, Samson to blindness and prison and Herakles to the underworld. Samson's menial labour in the prison has suggested the labours of Herakles at the order of the weaker Eurystheus. The episode of the Gates of Gaza has been compared to the setting up of the Pillars of Herakles, also a geographical feature and now the Strait of Gibraltar.

The possibility of Greek influence on Hebrew tradition in Palestine in the period of the Judges (about 1225–1050 B.C.) used to be doubted. But archaeology has now revealed Mycenaean settlements at Minet al-Beida, the coastal quarter of Ras Shamra, and at Tell Abu Hawam between Haifa and Akko. Nearer to the scene of the Samson story, the theme of the myth of Perseus and Andromeda, which has a Canaanite version in the abandoning of the goddess Astarte to the tyrant Sea, was localised at Jaffa. The influence in this case may have been rather of the Canaanite on the Mycenaean myth. But there is so much evidence of inter-relation of the two cultures at this time, that it is quite possible that the Samson tradition may have been influenced by the Herakles myth. Another mythological influence on the Samson tradition may have been the Gilgamesh legend. In this, as in the Samson cycle, females play a notable role. Ishtar, for instance, is the opponent of Gilgamesh and the wild man Enkidu is tamed by the harlot, as Samson was subdued and betrayed by Delilah to the Philistines. We do not suggest, however, that the Samson stories can be completely resolved into a series of myths. The story does probably reflect the activities of Nazirites, who were dedicated to resist alien influences. The story of Samson is told at such length in order to emphasise the disaster that follows the trifling with the solemn Nazirite vow. The grave of the hero between Zorah and Eshtaol and his tribal affinity surely indicate a nucleus of historical tradition.

We should emphasise that those are but a few selected instances of the elaboration of history in the Old Testament through myth. Space does not permit a full treatment of this subject, but only the citation of a few notable examples, which it is hoped may provide a guide to a critical appraisal of the historical material in the Pentateuch and the theological interpretation of the history of Israel in Joshua, Judges, Samuel and Kings, the Deuteronomic History.

Right: Bedouin watering goats and sheep in a well in the southern steppe, the main area of the desert wandering of the Israelites.

Below: the ancient site of Jericho looking southwards towards the Dead Sea, with the region of Qumran to the west and the land of Moab to the east.

The oldest festal calendars in Israel, Exodus 23.14–17, and the Ritual Code in Exodus 34.21–24, both from the period of the settlement in Palestine (about 1225-1050 B.C.), indicate the significance of the autumn festival of Tabernacles on the eve of the New Year and festivals at the two other important seasonal crises, the beginning of the barley harvest in April and the end of the wheat harvest seven weeks later, the festivals respectively of Unleavened Bread, associated with Passover, and Weeks, or Pentecost. The deliberate association of these with the Exodus, Covenant and Possession of the Promised Land at the central sanctuary of the sacral confederacy of Israel ('before the Lord') was contrived to counteract the natural tendency of the newcomers to observe the ritual of the seasonal crises of the local Canaanite peasants, which they considered as important as the new techniques of local agriculture.

THE FEAST OF TABERNACLES

The great autumn festival on the eve of the new year, '*the* festival' in Hebrew, was associated with periodic celebration by Israel of the Covenant-sacrament with its prelude in the Great Deliverance from Egypt. But it also remained an agricultural festival, retaining many local Canaanite features, notably the celebration of the Kingship of God won in conflict, and maintained against the menace of the powers of disorder, drought, sterility, death, the primeval forces of Chaos, the unruly waters Sea-and-Ocean Current, and the associated monster, the Primeval Serpent of Canaanite myth.

The liturgy of the Canaanite New Year festival with its central theme, the effective Kingship of God, was adapted in Hebrew religion, so that the influence of the God of Israel was extended to the sphere of nature. The narrow conception of the god of a particular militant tribal group was transformed into that of God as King, whose presence and power to sustain His government, or Order, against the menace of Chaos were experienced anew at each New Year festival. Thus through its origin in the liturgy of the Canaanite New Year festival, no theme in the Bible is more richly invested with the imagery of mythology than the Kingship of God.

Israel, in virtue of her experience of God as active in the crises of history and the moral sphere, transformed the Canaanite conception of the Kingship of God limited to the sphere of nature in the liturgy of the agricultural festival. This adaptation was facilitated by the fact that this was also the occasion when the Covenant sacrament with its historical prelude, the Great Deliverance from Egypt, was celebrated. Yet in psalms on the Kingship of God in the Old Testament, which may be demonstrated to be liturgies of the New Year festival (e.g. Psalms 46, 47 and 93), the mythological imagery of the Canaanite New Year liturgy remained, and also the central theme of God's 'showdown' with the forces of Chaos. Thus, as in the Baal myth at Ras Shamra, God's exaltation as King is signalised by thunder. His royal power is consummated, like that of Baal at Ras Shamra and Marduk in the New Year liturgy at Babylon, by the establishment of His 'house'. In the same context, God is 'He who mounts the clouds'. This epithet is one of the stock descriptions of Baal in the Ras Shamra texts. God's kingship, like that of Baal, is secured by His triumph over the unruly waters. A refinement of the Canaanite theme of the conflict of God and the waters is the victory of God by His word, or 'rebuke', a development of the conception of the thunder as

The Reign of God

Mount Hermon just beyond Israel, regarded as one of the seats of Baal-Hadad.

the voice of God and the expression of His power. God's triumph over the sea was easily transformed into the theme of His triumph over the Egyptians at the Sea of Papyrus Reeds, as for instance in Psalms 74.13, the more particularly as the Covenant with its historical prelude in the Great Deliverance was sacramentally celebrated at the New Year festival. The adversaries over whom God triumphs are usually depicted as sea-monsters. So God is praised in this context because he

shattered the heads of the dragons on the waters,
crushed the heads of Leviathan.

This is, of course, the monster familiar in the Ras Shamra mythology as the adversary of Baal:

. . . Lotan the Primeval Serpent,
. . . the Crooked Serpent,
The Close-coiling One with Seven Heads,

Isaiah 27.1 states:

On that day the Lord shall punish
With His great and strong sword
Leviathan the Primeval Serpent,
Leviathan the Crooked Serpent,
He will slay the dragon in the sea.

God's victory, as in the Babylonian New Year liturgy, is followed by creation (Psalms 74.15–17), which is a major theme in the great lyrics on the Sovereignty of God in Isaiah 40–55. Like Baal in the Canaanite liturgy, and surprisingly in a desert-deity, God's presence and ascendancy is signalised by rain (Psalms 65.11; 68.8–9), which is accompanied by lightning, as in Baal's advent as King in the Ras Shamra texts. Here again the imagery of the Canaanite liturgy of the New Year festival in the fertility cult is readily adapted to the Exodus and Covenant tradition in Israel, where the theophany of God at Sinai was traditionally fire (Deuteronomy 33.2).

The antagonists of God in this critical conflict might be identified in Israel with the historical enemies of God and His people (e.g. Psalms 47.3, 8), and the prophet Nahum (ch. 2–3) could exult in the downfall of Assyrian Nineveh as an instance of God's effective assertion of His Kingship in his contribution to the liturgy of the New Year festival, to which he clearly alludes in 1.15. Such passages afford convincing proof of the Kingship of God as the theme of the Feast of Tabernacles at the New Year season. This was 'the day of the Lord', the day of His decisive conflict with the forces of Chaos, when Israel would be again assured of His presence and His power to prevail over the forces of disintegration and Chaos. It was this annual experience that rallied Israel again and again in her hazardous situation among hostile neighbours and between the great imperial powers on the Nile and Euphrates. Yet this application of the ideology of the Kingship of God to the historical situation was fraught with danger. It might, and did, lead to a quite unspiritual chauvinism, as Amos apprehended (Amos 5.18–20). But, as Amos, Isaiah (ch. 2; 6) and Zephaniah (ch. 1) saw, the reality of the Kingship of God was a challenge to Israel herself.

GOD AS CREATOR

This theme of the Kingship of God, developed from the liturgy of the New Year festival in Israel's first contact with Canaan, is one of the central themes of the Bible, notably in the Psalms and Prophets in the Old Testament. It also stands in the forefront of the Gospel (Mark 1.15), where Jesus' miracles betoken God's establishment of His Order in creation; it is a theme also of the liturgy of the New Year festival in the Temple of Jerusalem, and of the Babylonian New Year liturgy. Creation as a manifestation of God's Order, or effective rule, in Hebrew thought, has been thought to be a borrowing from Mesopotamia in the period when Assyria dominated Palestine in the eighth and seventh centuries B.C. It may be observed that Baal, the liturgy of whose cult in the Canaanite New Year festival so strongly influenced the liturgy of the autumn festival in Israel, is not creator. In Canaanite mythology this was the province of El, the paramount god of the Canaanite pantheon. Now this was the god probably worshipped in Jerusalem before the Israelite occupation, El Elyon ('the Most High God'), mentioned in Genesis 14.18. Therefore, creation as an aspect of the Kingship of God in the New Year liturgy in the Temple may reflect the fusion in Israel of the two aspects of God already recognised in Canaan, the dynamic kingship represented by Baal and the permanent divine kingship of El the Creator. The social interest of the latter made the assimilation to the conception of the Covenant-God Yahweh the more easy, especially as the Covenant sacrament was celebrated also at the autumn festival on the eve of the New Year.

In the Old Testament, apart from obvious liturgies of the New Year festival in the Psalms and passages in the Prophets which reflect this, the motifs and imagery traditionally associated with the Kingship of God were sufficient to evoke to those familiar with the liturgy the whole ideology of the Kingship of God with all its implications. Two instances may suffice.

The passage in Isaiah 7.14, 'Behold a virgin shall conceive and bear a son and shall call his name Immanuel' is a case in point. The key to the understanding of this passage is 'Immanuel' ('God with us'), in which we recognise the theme of the refrain in Psalm 46, an Enthronement Psalm,

The Lord of Hosts is with us,
The God of Jacob is our refuge.

The Psalm depicts the exaltation of God and the establishment of His Order in despite of the menace of the forces of Chaos in nature and in history. Of Isaiah 7.14, it must first be stated that 'virgin' is a mistranslation of the Hebrew 'almah, which means in fact 'a young woman sexually mature', bearing or capable of bearing her first child, which signifies the early teens in the East. The context is that Isaiah in the name of God has assured King Ahaz in a political crisis, and has invited him to seek a sign, which would authenticate the assurance. A miracle, or spectacular portent, is clearly visualised by the prophet in his confidence that he speaks with the authority of God. On the King's refusal to ask such a sign, Isaiah himself adduces a 'sign', not a miracle, which will rebuke the King's pusillanimity. In 'Immanuel' he cites the refrain of Psalm 46 from the liturgy of the New Year festival, with its theme the advent of God as King to make His rule effective, and to sustain His purpose and His people against the menace of all the forces of Chaos and frustration. The message of the festival would, in fact, be appropriated even by young girls in their great ordeal of the first birth to the extent that they would name their children 'God with us'. Thereby they reproached the King who, as the executive of the Divine King, ought to have been the first to let the theme of the New Year festival govern his life.

JOB AND THE KINGSHIP OF GOD

In Wisdom literature the theme may recur either more or less completely, suggesting to those who were familiar with it in its traditional context the whole ideology of the Kingship of God. Thus Job, questioning God's ordered rule, with which the suffering of the innocent seems incongruous, asks, recalling the imagery of the Canaanite myth with its Hebrew adaptation,

Am I Sea or Tannin
That you set a guard over me? (Job 7.12)

(i.e. Is the innocent man no better than the inveterate enemy of God's Order?) So Eliphaz, contending for God's Order against Job's complaints, mentions God's providence in the rain (Job 5.9) as an introduction to a statement of His Order in society (Job 5.11–18). Job emphasises God's strange neglect of him, citing first the orthodox arguments for God's Order in the style of a Hymn of Praise to the Creator in the familiar convention of a series of statements of God's exploits in participial form, which culminates in the statement, which recalls Marduk's triumph over Tiamat (Job 9.13):

Under Him bow the champions of Rahab ('the Restless One', i.e. Sea).
In a similar Hymn of Praise to the Creator (Job 26.5–14), who
Binds up the waters in His clouds (v. 8)

and expresses His power, like Baal, in thunder (v. 14), Bildad argues for the Order and effective rule of God as King. God's exploits in this passage include the stilling of the sea and the piercing of the Primeval Serpent, both well-known in the Canaanite Baal myth on the subject of Divine providence. God also smites Rahab,

Breaking her in pieces by the winds of heaven,

recalling Marduk's triumph over Tiamat (the lower deep) in the Babylonian New Year Liturgy by bursting her with the winds (see p. 31).

Finally Elihu's arguments for the effective rule of God are rounded out by a Hymn of Praise (Job 36.26–37.13), which might well be an elaboration of the passage in the Baal myth of Ras Shamra, where Baal's thunder, lightning and rain signalise his establishment as King:

Lo, God is great beyond our knowledge,
The number of his years is unsearchable,
For he scoops up drops from the sea,
Distills them as rain for the abyss,
With which the clouds pour,
Dropping showers on the earth;
Yea, by these he feeds the peoples;
He gives food in abundance.

Can anyone understand how the clouds are spread out,
The crashing from His tabernacle?
Behold, the Most High spreads out His light,
And covers the tops of the mountains.

In His hands the lightning flashes,
He discharges it to a certain target;
His thunder announces His coming,
Showing zealous wrath against iniquity.
At this moreover my heart trembles
And starts out of its place.

Hear, O hear the turmoil of His thunder,
And the rumbling that comes from His mouth.
Under the whole sky is His flashing,
And His light to the edges of the earth.

In the wake of it His voice roars,
He thunders with His majestic voice,
And He does not restrain the water,
As peal upon peal is heard.

The Jordan by Jericho associated with the crossing of Israel in the Book of Joshua, and possibly the scene of a sacramental crossing in connection with the national worship at nearby Gilgal.

God does wondrous things,
He does great things beyond our ken,
For He commands the snow, 'Fall to the earth!'
And the downpour and the rain, 'Be strong!'

He seals up all human activity,
That every man may rest from his work;
And the wild beasts go to their lair,
And stay in their dens.

From the Chamber comes the whirlwind,
And from the Scatterers the cold.
By the Breath of God ice is made,
And the expanse of water is made solid.

Moreover His bright (sun) thrusts away the thick clouds,
Its light dispels the cloud.
And it goes on its course in its circuits,
Turning at its guidance,
To do all the work he commands it
On the face of the whole world.
Whether for chastisement or for favour,
Or as (a pledge of) steadfast grace, he makes it light upon one.

APOCALYPTIC LITERATURE

While the Kingdom of Judah still stood, the people of God retained their means of self-expression in the Temple in Jerusalem, with the king of the House of David as the representative of the people before God and as the executive of the Divine King, God's temporal guarantee of His sovereign power to sustain His Order. Thus they sustained their faith in God's purpose for Israel, particularly by the sacramental experience of the Sovereignty of God in the liturgy of the New Year festival. The little kingdom might feel the reverberations of the clash of the big battalions of the pagan world-powers, but she was reassured that in God's economy there was a 'thus far and no further' to the forces of Chaos. It was otherwise when Judah was no longer a sovereign kingdom, when there was no longer a reigning king as a visible assurance of the sovereignty of God.

In such circumstances it is a tribute to the tenacity of the Jewish faith that it continued to stay itself on the experience on which it had been traditionally fostered, the ideology of the Kingship of God in the New Year festival. Indeed, it seemed that this faith intensified in proportion as the visible tokens of the Divine support of Israel diminished. It was now that men of faith concentrated on cosmic perspectives and behind the façade of history won insights into God's execution of His ultimate purpose. They gave their contemporaries a glimpse beyond, discovering 'God behind the shadows', which is the significance of apocalyptic literature, a distinctive feature of Judaism in the last two centuries before Christ and the first of the Christian era. The apocalyptic works include the Book of Daniel (ch. 7–12) and the Book of Revelation in the Bible, and in the Apocrypha we shall draw mainly upon the Book of Enoch (c. 165–64 B.C.); the Testament of the Twelve Patriarchs (c. 109–106 B.C.); the Apocalypse of Baruch, the Syriac translation of the Greek, contemporary with the Gospels, Acts and Epistles of Paul (c. A.D. 50–90); and IV Ezra, or Esdras, known in Latin, Syriac, Ethiopic and Arabic from a Greek and possibly Hebrew original. This is a composite work, some of it roughly contemporary with Revelation; the compilation was completed by about A.D. 120.

Above: looking southwards from near Nazareth to Mount Gilboa, where Gideon mustered his commando for the attack on the Midianites (Judges 7), and Saul fought his last battle (1 Samuel 31). The upland plain just west of the end of the ridge of Gilboa is the Plain of Dothan, where Joseph was sold by his brothers (Genesis 37.17 ff.).

Left: a sounding trench in the excavation of Megiddo, looking northwards over the great central plain of Palestine, the scene of the victory of Barak and Deborah over Sisera (Judges 4 and 5).

This is a very complex field, in which it is impossible to systematise, for the authors, in spite of their intense devotion and insight, were still human and unable to disclose accurately or fully God's secrets. Hence there is no unanimity in details, the more so as so much concerns the hereafter beyond the grave, on which even Pharisees, who believed in the resurrection, were notoriously vague. Moreover, even in the pre-Exilic period a deep division had opened between man's interpretation of the implications of the establishment of God's reign. Popular belief eagerly anticipated God's vindication of His people in the realisation of nationalistic hopes. Wiser men, such as the prophets Amos and Isaiah of Jerusalem, saw that the imposition of the Order of the Divine King would involve catastrophe for many in Israel as well as for her Gentile opponents. In apocalyptic literature we find both aspects of the hope of the establishment of the Reign of God, one the vindication of

Israel and the ruthless crushing of her political enemies and the other the nobler, universalistic prospect of the final discomfiture of the forces of evil under their personal head, Satan or Belial. Nor are those aspects of the establishment of the Reign of God clearly separated in the literary sources. A single writer may be primarily interested in the suffering and frustration of God's people Israel while aware, before the Sovereignty of God, of the limitations of a purely national prospect. Or, like the writer in IV Ezra 3.4–36, he may be alive to the problem of the sin and suffering of mankind in general as a frustration of the purpose of the Creator.

In spite of the often bewildering diversity of the apocalyptic prospect, however, common features which we have already noticed as essential in the ideology of the Kingship of God expressed in the liturgy of the New Year festival in Mesopotamia, Canaan and Israel predominate. The recurrent pattern is the real and serious menace to the Order of the Divine King from the forces of Chaos, the vital conflict, the triumph of God and the vindication of His Kingship, and the imposition of His Order to the discomfiture of the forces of Chaos and the relief of all who put their trust in Him.

The liturgy of the Canaanite seasonal festival of autumn and New Year, from which the corresponding Hebrew festival was an adaptation, continues to influence this apocalyptic prospect. As the arrogant Sea-and-Ocean Current disputes the kingship of Baal in the Canaanite liturgy, so God's inveterate opponents are often described as the waters, for instance 'the black waters' in the Syriac Baruch 33.1–11. In Revelation 21.1, God's final triumph is signalised by 'a new heaven and a new earth' and 'there shall be no more sea' to dispute His reign. In Daniel 7.3, the various beasts, which symbolise opposition to the Order of God and the welfare of His people Israel, come up 'out of the sea', like the Roman eagle in IV Ezra 11. On the other hand, the executive of the Divine King, 'the Man' in IV Ezra 13.1, also comes up from the sea. The sea in this case symbolises the hostility of the forces of Chaos from which the agent of God has emerged triumphant–'He drew me out of many waters'. Or the arch-enemy may be depicted as a sea-monster, 'tannin', as in the Baal myth of Ras Shamra (see page 78), as the Roman general Pompey was described as tannina in the Syriac Psalm of Solomon. It is of further interest to note the persistence at this late date of the conception of thunder and lightning as symbolic of the ascendancy of God as King, as it had been of Baal at the height of his power as king in triumph over his enemies in the Ras Shamra texts. So in the Syriac Baruch 33.1–11 God's lightning triumphs over 'the black waters', converting them into beneficent rain and fertilising streams, and thunder and lightning herald the imposition of God's Order in Enoch 59.1–3 and the downfall of 'great Babylon' in Revelation 16.18.

As we have seen, the sacrament of the Sinai Covenant with its historical prelude in the Great Deliverance was associated with the New Year festival with its adaptation of the Canaanite New Year liturgy early in the Hebrew settlement of Israel in Palestine and throughout the Monarchy. So the circumstances of the Sinai theophany, fire, smoke and earthquake, herald the coming of God as King in Enoch 60.1 and Revelation 16.18; and the deliverance of Israel from Exile, a new Exodus, is part of the more nationalistic aspect of the apocalyptic prospect (Enoch 57.1–3; Song of Solomon 11).

God's decisive advent is described in the Old Testament as 'the Day of the Lord' or simply 'that day'. Certain passages use the imagery of warfare to describe this intervention of God, particularly the holy war in the days of Israel's settlement in Palestine described in the book of Judges. This imagery recurs in the description of the decisive advent of the Divine King in apocalyptic literature, especially during the period of the Roman domination of the Jews at the time of Christ. The earliest references in the Old Testament to 'the Day of the Lord' (Amos 5.18–20; Isaiah 2.11, 12, 17), however, indicate that it signified primarily the advent of God to vindicate His Kingship in conflict with the powers of Chaos in the great 'showdown' in the New Year festival. From Amos' pointed statement that the Day of the Lord would not be one of light, but darkness, we may conclude that it was associated with a light-ritual. This is reflected in Jesus' statement 'I am the Light of the world' in the context of the New Year Feast of Tabernacles, and in the torch-dance mentioned as an element in the ritual of this festival in the Babylonian Talmud. It has been suggested in fact that the advent of God, signalising anew His Kingship, was symbolised by the sun rising over the Mount of Olives to the east of Jerusalem to shine through the doors of the Temple into the inmost shrine, or 'Holy of Holies'.

God's kingly power is thus well symbolised as light shining in darkness, which did not overpower it (John 1.5). The darkness is the fitting symbol of the powers which seek to thwart His purpose, as in Egyptian mythology, which emphasised the daily conflict between the sun and Apophis, the dragon of darkness. Similar is the dragon in Revelation 12.4, which swept down a third of the stars and waited to engulf the Messianic child. There seems to be an echo of ritual conflict with the powers of darkness in the prospect of God's salvation 'as it turns to morning' in Psalms 46.5, with its theme of God's exaltation and His establishment of His Order against the menace of Chaos in nature and history in what we take to be part of the liturgy of the New Year festival. The theme of the conflict of light and darkness in God's final decisive advent is, of course, familiar in the Gospels and is the subject of the well-known text from the Sect of the New Covenant by the Dead Sea, the war of the Sons of Light with the Sons of Darkness. So in the consummation of the Reign of God 'there shall be no night' (Revelation 21.25).

A Christian interpretation of Jonah being cast to the 'whale'. Relief from a third-century A.D. sarcophagus.

THE TRIUMPH OF THE MESSIAH

We have already noticed the awareness of the apocalyptic writers to the problem of the sufferings of mankind as well as of the frustration of Israel as the people of God in an order where God was considered omnipotent. Thus sometimes they expect the decisive conflict in which the Messiah, or anointed executive of the Divine King, triumphs over the adversaries of his people, usually visualised as the political enemies of Israel; and sometimes they look for a temporary ascendancy of the Messiah and the people of God and a temporary suppression of the forces of evil, which varies in duration from 40, 70, and 365 years to 'three generations', 1,000 years (Revelation 20.2) and even, in the reckoning of a certain Rabbi, as long as from the creation of the world to his own time.

The establishment of the temporary Messianic kingdom and the later final consummation of the Reign of God are features also of the Christian apocalypse Revelation, especially 19.11, which, with due allowance for Christian adaptation, we may take as typical of apocalyptic in this respect. The Messiah appears with his robe emblazoned with the name 'the King of Kings and Lord of Lords' (19.11–16); the respective forces gather; 'the beast', the Roman oppressor, is captured and thrown into a lake of burning brimstone, and his forces are slain and devoured by the birds (19.17–21). The arch-enemy, the Devil ('the Accuser'), or Satan, visualised also, like the forces of Chaos in Canaanite and pre-Exile Hebrew liturgies from the New Year festival, as 'the dragon, that ancient serpent', is consigned to the bottomless pit, where he remains chained for a thousand years, so that the immediate objective, the realisation of a holy community like Israel, should be affected.

The establishment of God's Order is visualised also as a judgment: 'order', or 'government', and 'judgment' are both expressed by the same word. This is effected summarily by the discomfiture of the armies of Chaos and by a formal vindication of those who had been martyred for their faith without

Right: the ruins of Ahab's palace looking southward.

Opposite: mural painting from the synagogue at Dura Europus in northern Mesopotamia (second century A.D.). It depicts the Jewish interpretation of Ezekiel's vision of the revival of the dry bones (Exekiel 37).

seeing God's vindication (20.4–5). They are resurrected in 'the first resurrection' (20.5b), and are subjects of the Messianic kingdom for a thousand
years (20.6). After this period, Satan is released and gathers his forces
Gog and Magog from the remote parts of the earth for a final conflict. But
they are overcome by fire from heaven, presumably another case of the
lightning as an expression of God's sovereignty and ability to maintain His
Order. The Devil is thrown to his final doom in the lake of fire, where, with
'the beast' and 'the false prophet', he will suffer eternal torment.

A variation on this theme is the death of the Messiah and all his subjects
after the Messianic interim and the relapse of everything into a primeval
silence, pending a new creation of heaven and earth with a fiery hell, Gehenna,
an infernal ash-pit, so-called after the refuse dump of ancient Jerusalem in
the Valley of Hinnom to the south-west of the city. Reward for virtue is a
new Garden of Eden. In Revelation also there is a final judgment at which the
sinners are resurrected and find that death has not frustrated God's justice,
for they are consigned to torment in the lake of fire and brimstone (20.11–15)
in the 'second death' (21.8). The people of God on the other hand are settled
in peace and perpetual light (21.25; 22.5) in the new Jerusalem, the building
and paving of which glow with precious stones. The theme of the undisturbed
peace and blessing in the Kingdom of God is further developed in the motif
of the Garden of Eden with its source of living water and the Tree of Life,
with which the ancient Sumerians, Amorites and Assyrians were familiar.
We have seen that this was a part of the local mythology of Jerusalem, probably
from pre-Israelite times. It was developed in the motif of the Garden of
Eden with its wellhead of four rivers and its Tree of Life (Genesis 2.4–14):

Then he showed me the river of the water of life, bright as crystal, flowing from
the throne of God and of the Lamb through the middle of the street of the city;
also on either side of the river, the tree of life with its twelve kinds of fruit, yielding
its fruit each month; and the leaves of the tree were for the healing of the nations.
(Revelation 22.1–2)

We have noticed that the vindication of the people of God, whether Israel or the Christian Church, with the discomfiture of those outside, was of itself an intolerable limitation to the Reign of God. This prompted the conception of a second creation, in which the initial purpose of God should be fulfilled with no frustration. So in the final consummation, glimpsed by the prophets (e.g. Isaiah 2.2–4; 42.1–4), the bringing of mankind into the state of bliss in the Kingdom of God is the final hope of apocalyptic literature, so beautifully expressed in Revelation 21.23–24:

And the city has no need of sun or moon to shine upon it, for the glory of God is its light, and its lamp is the Lamb. By its light shall the nations walk; and the kings of the earth shall bring their glory into it.

Compare the conception of the new Garden of Eden and the Tree of Life, with its leaves 'for the healing of the nations' (Revelation 22.2).

THE DEVELOPMENT OF SATAN

It is symptomatic of this appreciation of the cosmic or universal nature of the conflict for the Reign of God that the inveterate enemies of the Divine King, though often particularised as the political enemies of Israel and symbolised in the imagery of Mesopotamian and Canaanite liturgies as arrogant waters, or sea monsters, became eventually a hierarchy under the personal leadership of the Devil.

As the arch-enemy of God and man who strives to thwart the purpose of God in the noblest of His works, we are familiar with Satan, the Devil of the New Testament, *Paradise Lost*, Dante's *Inferno* and Goethe's *Faust*, or Beelzebul ('Prince Baal'), parodied as Beelzebub ('Lord of Flies') of Jewish apocalyptic. As the fallen angel Lucifer of *Paradise Lost*, which is derived from 'the Bright One, Son of the Dawn' (Isaiah 14.12 ff), he is cast down from the zenith to the underworld. Satan gained an established place in late Jewish and Christian thought to explain the sinister reality of sin and suffering in a world which faith believed to be under the wise and beneficent guidance of Almighty God. The conception of him in his dual aspect of the enemy of God and man and fallen angel may be traced back to origins in mythology.

Satan, in this character, is a late development in Judaism, not appearing until the Books of Chronicles in the third century B.C. (1 Chronicles 21). In the monarchic period in Israel (c. 1000–586 B.C.) in fact such a figure as a rival to God is intolerable. Suffering and calamity were considered to be directly sent or permitted by God. From her emergence as a distinctive sacral community committed to the worship of her God alone, Israel had come to terms with the current polytheism of the Near East. While not worshipping other gods, she recognised their worship by other peoples. Thus in the Song of Moses (Deuteronomy 32.8) we read the statement:

When the Most High assigned the peoples their portion,
When He separated the sons of men,
Fixing the bounds of the peoples,
According to the number of the sons of El,
Yahweh's portion was His people,
Jacob the lot of His inheritance.

These gods, however, are regarded in Israel as inferior to the God of Israel. The conception of a divine assembly, or council, is borrowed from Mesopotamia and Canaan in Psalm 82.1, but only to serve as the scene for God's

formal indictment of the moral ineffectiveness and injustice of the other gods. This process reaches its logical conclusion in the condemnation of other gods as useless images (Psalm 135. 15–18), mere stocks and stones (Isaiah 44.9–20), and in the overthrow of 'the host of heaven' with 'the kings of the earth' in the day of God's advent as King and their consignment to the pit in the apocalyptic passage in Isaiah 24.21–23.

On the other hand, the conception of the divine assembly was developed in the conception of the heavenly court composed of the God of Israel and other celestials as His assessors and executors, as in Psalms 89.19–21. Chronologically this stage is illustrated by the passage in 1 Kings 22.19–28, when the prophet Micaiah reported a vision of the Lord summoning one of the heavenly court ('the heavenly host') to seduce the prophets who were encouraging Ahab to go to his doom. A similar conception is expressed in the prologue to the Book of Job (Job 1.6–2: 8), where God in His celestial assembly ('the sons of God') reviews mankind. One of this assembly is 'the *satan*', who questions the disinterested character of Job's righteousness and is given leave to put it to the test. Here, in spite of English translations, the figure is not yet Satan the inveterate enemy of God and man. He is an executive of God, one of the 'sons of God', who combines the office of an intelligence agent, with a suggestion of *agent provocateur* and public prosecutor, as in the vision of the prophet Zechariah (3.1–3), where the only suggestion of the sinister role is his excess of zeal. This contrasts with the more positive role of executives of God in His purpose with man, which is played by personal angels who intercede for men (Job 33.23 ff).

In 1 Chronicles 21 (c. 300 B.C.), in contrast to the statement in the parallel passage in Samuel that God had sent a plague in consequence of David's census, it is said that Satan rose up against Israel and incited David to take the census of the people with the fatal consequences. The development of the conception of Satan as the personal power of evil, who had his counterpart in the archangel Michael, the champion of the cause of man in God's purpose of creation, was probably developed under the influence of Persian Zoroastrian belief in the two conflicting spirits of good and evil, respectively Ahuramazda and Angramainyu, and their angelic hierarchies. The Manual of Creed and Conduct of the Sect of the New Covenant by the Dead Sea suggests that the sect was involved in an imminent war between the two angelic forces.

While Persian influence cannot be denied, the continual conflict of God and the forces of evil in nature and in history and the forces of moral chaos was of course long familiar in Israel, being the theme of the New Year festival. In this supreme conflict for the Kingship, or government, the antagonists of God are often spoken of in the Hebrew liturgy as 'the kings', or 'kings and nations', and the association of 'the kings of the earth' in Isaiah 24.21–23 with 'the host of heaven' to be punished 'on that day' indicates that the heathen gods are treated as the powers of Chaos. In the Canaanite version we have seen that the forces of Chaos which threaten the Kingship of Baal are sometimes identified with the Primeval Serpent, as they are in the liturgy of the New Year festival in Israel. This is the basis for the identification of Satan, or the Devil, with the serpent which tempted Eve and deceived the whole world and with his angels was thrown down from heaven by the archangel Michael and his angels (Revelation 12.7 ff.).

The conception of Satan as a fallen angel, Lucifer of *Paradise Lost*, may be traced from Isaiah 14.12–20:

How thou hast fallen from heaven,
O Bright One, Son of Dawn!
Thou art cut down to the ground,
More weak than all peoples.
Thou it was who said in thy heart,
'I will ascend to heaven;
Above the stars of God
I will set my throne on high;
Yea, I will be enthroned on the mount of assembly
On the highest parts of Saphon;
I will surmount the tops of the clouds,
I will be like the Most High.'
But thou art brought down to Sheol,
To the depths of the Pit.
Those who see thee will stare at thee,
They will ponder over thee:
Is this the man who made the earth tremble,
Who shook kingdoms,
Who made the world like a desert,
And ruined cities,
Who did not let his captives go?
. . . . . .
. . . kings of the nations
All of them lie in honour,
Each in his own home,
But thou art cast out away from thy grave,
Like loathed pollution,
Clothed like the slain, those pierced with the sword,
Who go down to the foundations of the Pit,
Like a dead body trodden under foot,
Thou shalt not be joined with them in burial.
Because thou hast destroyed thy land,
Thou hast slain thy people.

This taunt on the downfall of the king of Babylon, which is to be dated to the end of the Neo-Babylonian period (c. 539 B.C.), is a development of the passage in the Baal myth of Ras Shamra, which describes the inadequacy of Athtar, well known among the Arabs as the bright Venus star which signalises dawn and nightfall, to fill the throne of Baal on Mount Saphon in his absence. This is the prototype of Lucifer, the day star.

In a comparative study such as this, it is easy to emphasise common features to the exclusion of local differences, which may be no less impressive. This has been the fault of a good deal of work on the status and function of the king in the ancient Near East and particularly Israel. But here, as in other cultural and spiritual areas, the distinctive experience of Israel defies the effort to bring her institutions into conformity to a general Near Eastern culture-pattern.

THE SACRAL COMMUNITY OF ISRAEL

Israel took her origin as a sacral confederacy of kinship units on the basis of an act of Divine power and grace to which all men in the confederacy were debtors and which rendered all equally deserving of consideration. This condition was safeguarded by the renewal of the solidarity of the sacral community in the sacrament of the Covenant, when the religious and social obligations under Divine authority were regularly declared and accepted. Authority in such a community was vested in people who had given visible token of their insight into the will of God, like Samuel; or of their capacity for generous response to the call of God and total commitment to His purpose, like the great judges. This experience was recognised as possession by the spirit of God, which was authenticated by the manifest success of the leader, who was in consequence publicly recognised. Thus the first king, Saul, came to be recognised, and David after him, who was formally accepted as king first over Judah (2 Samuel 2.4) and then over Israel (2 Samuel 5.3) by the consent of the communities of each.

This public acclamation of the king by the sacral community continued in the monarchy in northern Israel, where occasionally the king was marked out by prophetic support, as were Jeroboam I, Jehu, and probably Baasha, though the custom was suspended under the hereditary feudal monarchy of the House of Omri, and towards the end of the kingdom in the eighth century B.C., when kings were either political opportunists raised by local parties or Assyrian vassals. In the southern kingdom of Judah under the House of David in Jerusalem the democratic spirit of the local elders reasserted the traditional right of the sacral assembly to confirm the king's authority by their acclamation at various crises in the monarchy, generally where the king's acknowledgment of responsibility to the God of Israel threatened to be ignored. Thus there was no single pattern of kingship in Israel which reflected the ideology of kingship which we have noticed in Mesopotamia and Canaan.

THE KING AS EXECUTIVE OF THE DIVINE KING

Nevertheless, we cannot fail to notice certain significant features in the conception of kingship in the House of David. David and his successors proposed to reign as the executive of the Divine King. This is clearly implied in their designation as the Servant, and even the Son, of God (Psalms 2; Isaiah 9.6), by their recognition of the obligations of God's covenant with David and his House, and by the commission of the king to be the agent of the Divine King in the conflict with the forces of Chaos and the imposition of His Order (Psalms 2 and 110). Set apart as uniquely associated with God by the right of anointing, the Davidic King is signalised as being set enthroned at the right hand of God, admitted to share His purpose and take measures to carry it into effect. Like kings in Mesopotamia and Canaan, he had the

The King and the Messiah

Divine commission to maintain social order and justice and was expected to be a father to the poor and weak, who depended on God and His executive for the recognition of their rights. He was the medium of material blessings, fertility and harmony in nature.

Other texts indicate the king as the unique intermediary between God and the community; for instance, in rites of penance in the fast-liturgy as in Mesopotamia. The most notable of these texts are Psalms 80 and 89. The latter, a composite psalm, though in its totality a fast-liturgy, opens with a reference to God's covenanted pledge to David, thereafter praising God in a Hymn of Praise to God as King triumphant over the sea and monsters of Chaos. God's Order is particularised in His choice of David as His vice-regent and the executive of the Divine power over forces of Chaos in history. All this is a foil to the present discomfiture of God's people concentrated in the humiliation of the king, and the psalm closes with the invocation of God's covenant with the House of David. The significance of the king in fast-liturgies, here explicit, probably underlies many other Plaints of the Sufferer in the Psalms where the reference to afflictions as unruly waters has suggested a role like the king's humiliation in the Babylonian New Year liturgy. Explicit evidence for this feasible view, however, is admittedly lacking.

Psalms 80 and 89 are in themselves a striking illustration not only of the status and function of the king as the executive of the Divine King, but also of his function as representative of the people in rites of fast and penance. The former aspect of the office of the king was emphasised in later political Messianism, the latter in the more positive, less spectacular Messianic hope of a minority, which found expression in the prophetic circle from which the great Servant Song in Isaiah 52.13–53.12 developed, with its realisation in the sufferings and death of Christ.

This ideal of kingship, which under its nobler exponents emphasised the responsibilities of royalty, which was not incongruous with the social obligations of the Covenant, was probably fostered by David to secure his dynasty against the uncertainties of popular favour. Unpopularity might be a hindrance to progress in a developing state. He was also anxious to safeguard ancestral tradition. There were doubtless many modifications to this royal ideology of Judah, and it must be remembered that all the evidence for it comes probably from the liturgy of the New Year festival, which emphasises the sacral, as distinct from the political, aspects of the Davidic kingship. Nevertheless it represents the view of the kingship in Judah which came to be commonly accepted Thus, for instance, in the Lamentations for the downfall of Jerusalem the king is lamented as

The breath of our nostrils, the Lord's anointed,
(Lamentations 4.20)

and in the philosophy of the history of Israel compiled by theologians from the end of the monarchy to *c.* 550 B.C., the vicissitudes of the people are related to the personal relationship of the king with God.

THE DAVIDIC MESSIAH

David firmly grounded his office and his dynasty in the association with the God of Israel expressed in the convention of the Divine covenant with him and his house, and in the various aspects of the king as the executive of the

Divine King which were publicly brought to notice in the regular worship at the central shrine in Jerusalem. As a result, even after the collapse of the state of Judah in 586 B.C. and until the resettlement of Jerusalem under the high priest seventy years later, men never abandoned hope of the revival of the political power of Judah under a survivor of the Davidic House. In subsequent ages, when the Jews had quite lost sovereign status, in face of the frustration of their destiny as God's covenanted people by the suppression of the Greek rulers of Syria in the third and second centuries B.C. and later by Rome, their faith in their destiny in the purpose of God was rallied by a development of the traditional theme of the New Year festival, the highlight of the religious year, when the Kingship of God and His Order were sustained against the menace of all the forces of Chaos.

A modification of this Messianic prospect was the hope of a Messiah not of the House of David, but of the House of Levi. This may reflect conditions after the revival of the Jewish community following the Exile under the high priest, or it may reflect the restoration of the monarchy under the Hasmonaeans, who were a Levitical family and not of Davidic descent. There is, however, no unanimity among scholars as to whether those two conceptions of the Messiah represent difference of opinion among contemporaries or whether the conception of the Davidic Messiah was revived after disappointment in the Hasmonaean House and its eventual fall.

Ivory border plaque for furniture inlay (ninth century B.C.), with motif of the Tree of Life and a palm with Egyptian lotus-flowers, both emblems of life and fertility. From the palace of Ahab at Samaria.

The Sect of the New Covenant by the Dead Sea looked to two Messiahs, one the Messiah of Aaron and the other the Messiah of Israel. They obviously visualised respectively sacral and secular figures rather than representatives of given families, though the Sect evidently believed in a Messiah of the Davidic House. In the New Testament, however, following more strictly the fulfilment of Old Testament promise in the Davidic covenant, there is no belief in any Messiah but the descendant of David. And as the reigning king of the House of David, 'God's anointed one', had been regarded as the executive of the Divine purpose, so now men continued to look for a scion of David as the executive of God and a visible guarantee of His power to effect His order. This figure is the Davidic Messiah of apocalyptic hope, which was realised for the Christian faith in Jesus Christ, i.e. the 'Anointed'.

Christian tradition takes extraordinary pains to emphasise the Davidic descent of the carpenter of Nazareth, while emphasising also the creative transformation of nature in the miracles as tokens of the immediate Divine activity. This reflects the curious tendency in Judaism, while hoping for the realisation of the supernatural Order of God, to impose national and local limitations and to identify the Messiah with historical figures, such as John Hyrcanus the Hasmonaean high priest and ruler (133–103 B.C.), the rebel leader Simon bar Koseba (died 135 A.D.) and others of less note. Thus the Messiah fulfils, in apocalyptic hope, the function of the former anointed kings of the House of David as the agent of the Divine King in realising His Order, as a warrior who suppresses the enemies of God and His people, an inexorable judge to them, and the champion of the right. He is one who, like the king in Isaiah 11.12 ff., will have supernatural wisdom and understanding, insight into God's purpose and effective power to carry it out, to judge the wicked and vindicate the right.

In the wonderful passage on the 'new priest' in the Testament of Levi (18.1–14), which refers to the priest-ruler John Hyrcanus, but, like Isaiah 9.27 and 11.1–9, applies to his office independently of personal limitations, the Messiah would be the medium of the revelation of the will of God in society, resulting in honesty and justice. He would, moreover, mediate knowledge of God's will to the Gentiles like the Servant of the Lord in Isaiah 42.1–4; 49.6 with a much more positive aim than mere victory in arms; indeed, by some means not disclosed he was to rehabilitate mankind (Testament of Levi 18.10):

And he shall open the gates of Paradise,
He shall remove the threatening sword against Adam.

With the declaration (16.11):

He shall give the saints to eat of the Tree of Life,

there is an interesting reversion to the motif of the king as the tender of the Tree of Life in the Garden of God, with which we became familiar among the Sumerians, Amorites and Assyrians in Mesopotamia, with its variant in Canaan and Israel in the conception of the king as the dispenser of fertility. So in the Syriac Baruch 73.2–74.1, with the advent of the Messiah

Healing shall descend in dew
And disease shall withdraw,
And judgments and revilings and contentions and revenge,
And blood and passions and envy and hatred,
And whatsoever things are like these
Shall go into condemnation when they are removed,
And no one shall die untimely,
Nor shall any adversity suddenly befall.
And wild beasts shall come forth from the forest
And minister unto men,
And asps and dragons shall come forth from their holes
To submit themselves to a little child;
And women shall no longer have pain when they bear;
And it shall come to pass in those days
That the reapers shall not grow weary,
Nor those that build be toilworn.

This vision obviously elaborates those aspects of the royal ideology described in Isaiah 11.1–9 and is strikingly realised in the ministry of Jesus Christ with its healing miracles and dynamic social gospel betokening God's rehabilitation of man in nature and in society. An interesting development of the theme of the restoration of harmony in nature by the Messiah is the representation in early Christian art of Christ as Orpheus, who charmed all beasts and even inanimate nature by his music.

THE MESSIANIC BANQUET
The conception of the Messianic banquet with his people after his triumph is what is known in anthropology as a rite of aggregation, signifying re-integration after the temporary suspension of normal order in a crisis. The

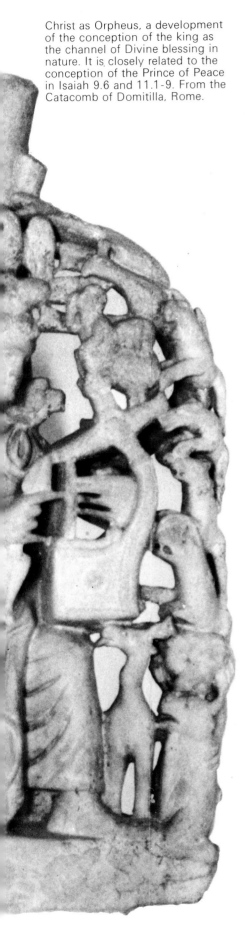

Christ as Orpheus, a development of the conception of the king as the channel of Divine blessing in nature. It is closely related to the conception of the Prince of Peace in Isaiah 9.6 and 11.1-9. From the Catacomb of Domitilla, Rome.

Messianic banquet has a precedent in the feast of Baal after his establishment as king when his palace is completed, which in turn has its counterpart in Solomon's great communion-sacrifice and public feast when the Temple was completed (1 Kings 8.62–66). This conception is found also in the Christian eschatological hope. A curious variation in Jewish apocalyptic is that the substance of this feast will be the flesh of Behemoth and Leviathan. In IV Ezra 6.53–54 it is noted that these represent respectively the beasts and reptiles created on the sixth day of creation just before the creation of man, who was to have dominion over them. There may, however, be mythical overtones. Leviathan is the Hebrew version of Canaanite *lôtan*, known in the Ras Shamra texts as one of the monsters of primeval Chaos which had sought to defy Baal as King,

Lotan the Primeval Serpent,
The Close-coiling One of Seven Heads.

In Job 40.15–24 and 41, where Behemoth, the hippopotamus, and Leviathan, the crocodile, are cited as creatures which defy the power and skill of man, those mythical overtones must be understood, though the primary reference is natural. It may be noted that in Egyptian myth and ritual, the hippopotamus symbolised the god Seth, the sinister power of disorder and destruction in the nature-cult at Edfu. It is then peculiarly fitting that the Messianic banquet after the triumph over the forces of Chaos should be furnished by the flesh of those creatures.

The figure of the Messiah as the son of David, however, had natural limitations; he was primarily the vindicator of God's purpose with Israel, and his reign was temporary until the final consummation, the new creation and the rehabilitation of mankind. So his limitation was recognised by the conception of his death (IV Ezra 7.29) together with all his followers and the reversion to the first beginning before creation preceding the resurrection to final judgment.

THE SON OF MAN

Like 'Messiah', the 'son of Man' is a royal title derived from the ideology of the king of the House of David during the Monarchic period in Judah, where it is attested in the royal Psalm 80.17 from the liturgy of the fast, where it stands parallel to 'the man of thy right hand', obviously the king, who was enthroned at the right hand of God. The 'Son of Man' takes us back to the old Mesopotamian conception of the king as the representative of the community tending the Tree of Life in the Garden of God, which symbolises at once man's service of God and the king as the mediator of God's blessing in nature to the community. The Mesopotamian conception of the king tending the Tree of Life in the Garden of God has been democratised in the Hebrew conception of Man in the Garden of Eden with its Tree of Life. But the denunciation of the king of Tyre in Ezekiel 28.12–19 as the executive of God, His signet, in 'the Garden of God' probably reproduces the conception of the king as the archetypal man in the Garden of God, of which the conception of Adam in the Garden of Eden, created in the image of God, is a theological democratisation. The recognition of the royal status of Man in the Garden of God and the known fact of the Son of Man as a title of the Davidic King explain the significance of the Son of Man in the apocalyptic prospect.

The figure appears in Jewish apocalyptic first in Daniel 7.9–14, where, in a judgment scene, after the parade of beasts 'coming up out of the sea', thus symbolising the forces of Chaos particularised in the pagan world-empires which had frustrated the purpose of God for Israel, 'one like a son of man' appears. This description emphasises his likeness to God in distinction from the brute figures, to which he is superior, conceptions both emphasised in the description of Adam ('Man') in Genesis 1.26. Therefore, the 'son of man' in Daniel 7.13 denotes God's people, who share His purpose.

According to the ancient Semitic conception of corporate personality, however, this does not exclude an individual leader, natural or supernatural. A supernatural leader, moreover, seems to be indicated by the note on the 'one like a son of man' coming 'with the clouds of heaven'. This became a characteristic of the conception of the supernatural Son of Man as the executive of the Divine King in the apocalyptic prospect of Judaism in the time of Christ. Jesus refers to the consummation of the present world order with the advent of 'The Son of Man coming on the clouds of heaven with power and great glory', a reference which was not lost on the high priest who condemned Jesus (Matthew 26.65; Mark 14.63). The imagery of the advent of the Son of Man on the clouds is probably borrowed from the enthronement psalms, where God is described as 'the rider on the clouds'. This in turn, of course, is an adaptation of the description of Baal, the divine king dynamic in the liturgy of the Canaanite New Year festival, as 'He who mounts the clouds'. The transference of the imagery to the Son of Man reflects the development of the conception of God as transcendent in late Judaism, where His more immediate activity is discharged by His angels or, in this case, by His executive, the supernatural Son of Man.

Apart from the New Testament, the Son of Man is known particularly from the section in the Book of Enoch known as the Similitudes, or Parables (ch. 37–71). Certain passages describe the Son of Man as the agent of God's wrath on His enemies, which suggests the identity of the Son of Man, who is also called the Elect, or Chosen, One, and the Messiah. He is certainly a royal figure, as is indicated by the references to 'the throne of his glory'. His reign shall also guarantee the welfare of the righteous. The Son of Man, therefore, seems a variant of the conception of the Messiah of apocalyptic hope, and, like the Messiah, is a development of the ideology of the king as the executive of the Divine King. The title may emphasise his function as the representative of his people, though of course not excluding his function as the mediator of the Divine purpose and power. In view of Jesus' preference for the title in reference to His own mission, it is tempting to take it as denoting the rehabilitation of mankind by the Messianic king as the archetypal Man, 'the last Adam' of 1 Corinthians 15.45. There is perhaps special reference to the representation of His people in vicarious suffering, as is suggested by Jesus' disclosure of his passion on Peter's confession 'Thou art the Messiah (Greek Christ)' (Mark 8.29; Luke 9.20). For this, however, there is no evidence in apocalyptic sources as distinct from the New Testament. Nor is it clear if the Son of Man, as distinct from the Messiah, is particularly associated with the final establishment of the Reign of God as distinct from the first, temporary settlement, in spite of the declaration of the universalistic hope (Enoch 48.4):

And he shall be the light of the Gentiles
And the hope of those who are troubled of heart.

Since the dawn of religious conscience in Mesopotamia three thousand years before Christ, myth had introduced men to the activity of God as Divine King in His own dimension, and the ideology of sacral kingship was an assurance of God's good will to effect His purpose for men, first through the reigning king as their representative as well as the executive of the Divine King and eventually in Judaism by the Messiah and the Son of Man. In this realm of eternal prospects, the dynamic Divine truths were beyond presentation in the prosaic language of daily life, and the symbolism of ritual supplemented by the dramatic narrative of myth with its rich imagery and symbolic figures effected the bridge between man's hopes and aspirations and the assurance of God.

For the Christian faith the Reign of God guaranteed by the executive of the Divine King, the Messiah, or Anointed One, and the Son of Man was effected through Jesus Christ. In Him those great themes became no longer the substance of myth, but of history. Their significance is the subject of theological interpretation. But theology, in discoursing on the great subjects of the Reign of God and the Messiah and the Son of Man, may devise its own idiom and imagery, its own 'mythology' in fact, which may strangely distort the native idiom of Jesus and his contemporaries in its very anxiety to be relevant and intelligible to later ages. Modern 'demythologising' brings its own perplexities and may well result in the great truths it seeks to elucidate becoming intelligible only to a limited circle inducted into the jargon of its own exponents and only to a certain age and theological tradition.

By comparison one may ask if we should not seek rather to understand the traditional idiom and imagery of the mythology of the ancient Near East and to arrive at a sympathetic appraisal of the hopes and prospects of men which they cherished in all earnestness in Mesopotamia, Canaan and Israel, until they were realised according to their own idiom in the fullness of time in Jesus Christ. This seems to the writer a safer way to objective truth, which may minimise variations in the theological interpretation of the person and office of Christ, and to this end he ventures to hope that this study of mythology in the ancient Near East may serve a sober and constructive purpose.

Proto-Ionic capital, a development of the stylised palm, the Tree of Life, so common in palace architecture in the Semitic East. Possibly from Solomon's palace in Jerusalem.

Troy

Hattushash

HATTI

Tarsus

Carch

Rhodes

Ugarit
(Ras Shamra)

Orontes

Cyprus

Hamath

Arvad

SYRIA

MEDITERRANEAN SEA

Byblos

PHOENICIA

Sidon

Damascus

Tyre

Jordan

PALESTINE

Rabbah of the Amm

Lachish

Jerusalem

Gaza

Nile Delta

EGYPT

Upper Egypt

ARABAH

Memphis

MIDIAN

Nile

Sinai

RED SEA

Thebes

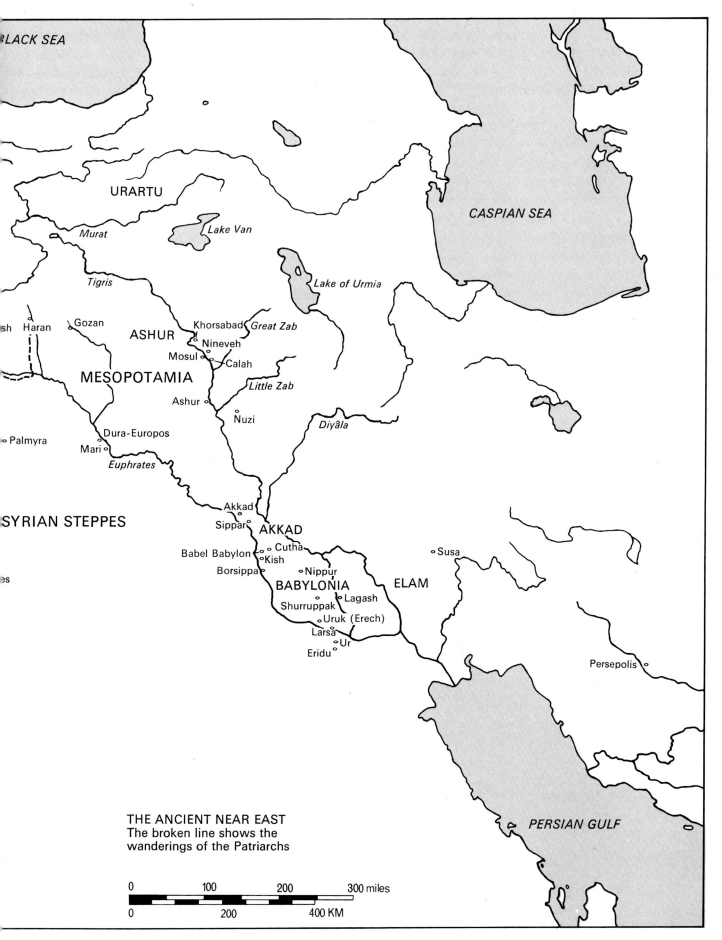

BLACK SEA

URARTU

Murat

Lake Van

CASPIAN SEA

Tigris

Lake of Urmia

sh Haran Gozan

Khorsabad *Great Zab*

ASHUR Nineveh

Mosul Calah

MESOPOTAMIA *Little Zab*

Ashur

Nuzi *Diyâla*

Palmyra Dura-Europos

Mari

Euphrates

SYRIAN STEPPES Akkad

Sippar AKKAD

Babel Babylon Cutha Susa

Borsippa Kish

Nippur ELAM

BABYLONIA

Shurruppak Lagash

Uruk (Erech)

Larsa Ur

Eridu Persepolis

PERSIAN GULF

THE ANCIENT NEAR EAST
The broken line shows the
wanderings of the Patriarchs

0	100	200	300 miles

0	200	400 KM

CHRONOLOGY OF THE HISTORY AND LITERATURE OF THE ANCIENT NEAR EAST

| | Political Events | | Literature | |
DATE	MESOPOTAMIA	SYRIA AND PALESTINE	MESOPOTAMIA	SYRIA AND PALESTINE
c. 3400-3300	Settlement of Sumerians		Invention of writing on clay tablets	
c. 2900	First Dynasty of Ur			
c. 2500-2400	Classical Sumerian period		Earliest Summerian literature	
c. 2300-2150	Old Akkadian period		Semitic Old Akkadian written in Sumerian script	
2100	Iranian invasions			
c. 2000-1900	Third Dynasty of Ur		Sumerian Renaissance, many new texts	
c. 1900-1800	Isin-Larsa hegemony; Amorite settlement			
c. 1750-1550	Old Babylonian (Amorite) period		Most Sumerian literature known from copies of this period	
c. 1500-1400	Cassite (Iranian) domination of south Mitannian (Hurrian and Aryan) domination of north		Editing of old texts, translation into Akkadian; new texts	
c. 1400-1300		Apogee of Canaanite culture on Syrian coast. Mycenaean (Aegean) settlement on Syrian coast		Myths and legends of Ras Shamra in alphabetic cuneiform
c. 1225		Decisive phase of Hebrew settlement in Palestine		
c. 1100	Rise of Assyria			
c. 1000-900		House of David ruled all Israel until 931, and in Judah till 586	Assyrian copies of Babylonian texts	First main narrative source of the Pentateuch compiled (c. 900)
c. 900-700	Aramaeans settle in centre and south; height of the Assyrian Empire		Collection of Library of Ashurbanipal	Earlier Hebrew Psalms (c. 950-586). First compilation of narratives of the Hebrew settlement (Joshua 2-11 and Judges); story of the Davidic Succession
c. 600-539	Neo-Babylonian Empire (Aramaean)			Compilation of the Deuteronomic History (Joshua, Judges, Samuel, Kings) c. 550
539-331	Persian period			
c. 300-100	Seleucid (Hellenistic) period		Berossus' Greek account of ancient myths	Final recension of Pentateuch Completion of compilation of Prophets
c. AD 36	Roman period			

Acknowledgments

The publishers gratefully acknowledge the following sources for permission to reproduce the illustrations indicated:

Colour Ashmolean Museum: 35; British Museum: 26-27, 69 top, 69 bottom; J. Allan Cash: 64-65; Giraudon: 27, 30 right, 53, 57, 60 bottom; Hirmer Fotoarchiv: 56, 60 top, 61, 85, 88, 89, 96, jacket; Middle East Archive: 30 left, 93, 109 top, 116, 124, 125; Oriental Institute, University of Chicago: back jacket; Uni-Dia: 109 bottom; Professor Yigael Yadin, The Hebrew University of Jerusalem: 92-93; Ziolo-Held: 113.

Black and White Archaeological Museums of Istanbul: 22-23 bottom: Bildarchiv Foto Marburg: 24, 63 bottom left, 98-99; British Museum: 12-13 top, 14 top, 16-17, 19 top, 19 centre, 20 top left, 33, 36, 41, 47, 58 bottom, 68, 73 bottom right, 74 top, 126, 127; J. Allan Cash: 67 bottom, 95, 102-103, 106, 110 bottom, 114 bottom, 119, 121 top, 121 bottom; Maurice Chuzeville: 63; J. E. Dayton: 73 top right, 132-133; Directorate General of Antiquities of Iraq, Baghdad: 20 top right, 22-23 top, 54 top, 78 left; Direction Générale des Antiquités et des Musées, Damascus: 71 top, 71 bottom, 90-91 top, 90-91 bottom, 101, endpaper; Ecole Biblique et Archéologique Française, Jerusalem: 110 top; Giraudon: 14 bottom, 16-17, 54 left, 59, 72, 74 bottom; Hamlyn Group Picture Library: 20 bottom, 73 bottom left; Hirmer Fotoarchiv: 6-7, 14 centre left, 21, 24-25, 52, 62 right, 63 top left, 104, 105; M. Holford: 42; Institut Français d'Archéologie, Beirut: 67 top, 67 centre; Institut Royal de Patrimoine Artistique—copyright A.C.L., Brussels: 107; Israel Department of Antiquities: 8, 70, 73 top left, 76 top left, 76 bottom left, 81, 82-83, 97 top, 97 bottom, 100 bottom, 100 top left; 131; Jerusalem Excavation Fund: 135; Koninklijk Penningkabinet, The Hague: 98 top, 98 centre; Mansell Collection: 18 bottom, 19 bottom, 38, 43, 44, 54 bottom right, 55 bottom, 77, 78 right; Middle East Archive: 114 top; National Museum, Beirut: 87, 100 right; Ny Carlsberg Glyptotek: 123; Oriental Institute of the University of Chicago: 28; Pierpont Morgan Library: 18 top, 29, 53; Service Photographique de la Réunion des Musées Nationaux, Versailles: 76; Staatliche Museen, Berlin: 55 top, 58 top; University Museum, Philadelphia: 62 left; Professor Yigael Yadin, The Hebrew University of Jerusalem: 94.

The photographs on pages 10-11, 12-13 bottom and 48 were taken by Wilfred Thesiger and are from his book *The Marsh Arabs*.

Further Reading List

GENERAL
Beek, M.A. *Atlas of Mesopotamia*, Nelson 1962
Grollenberg, L. *Atlas of the Bible*, Nelson 1957

MESOPOTAMIA
Contenau, G. *Everyday Life in Babylon and Assyria*, E. Arnold, 1954
Frankfort, H. *Kinship and the Gods*, Cambridge University Press, 1948
Hooke, S. H. *Babylonian and Assyrian Religion*, Hutchinson, 1953. ed. *The Labyrinth*, S.P.C.K., 1935. *Myth, Ritual and Kinship*, Oxford University Press, 1958.
Pritchard, J. B. (ed.), *Ancient Near Eastern Tests relating to the Old Testament*, Princeton University Press, 1954.
Saggs, H.W.F. *The Greatness that was Babylon*, Sidgwick and Jackson, 1962.

CANAAN
Contenau, G. *La Civilisation Phénicienne*, 1949.
Cork, S.A. *The Religion of Ancient Palestine in the Light of Archaeology*, Oxford University Press, 1930.
Driver, G.R. *Caanite Myths and Legends*, T and T Clark, 1956.
Dussaud, *Les Découvertes de Ras Shamra (Ugarit) et l'Ancien Testament*, 1937.
Gaster, T.H. *Thespis*, H. K. Lewis, 1950.
Gray, J. *The Legacy of Canaan*, E. J. Brill, Leiden, 2nd edition 1965. *The Canaanites*, Thames and Hudson, 1964.
Kapelrud, A.S. *Baal in the Ras Shamra Texts*, 1952. *The Violent Goddess*, 1964.
Schaeffer, C.F.A. *The Cuneiform Texts of Ras Shamra-Ugarit*, Oxford University Press, 1939

ISRAEL
Albright, W.F. *Archaeology and the Religion of Israel*, Oxford University Press, 3rd edition 1953
Bright, J. *A History of Israel*, SCM Press, 1960.
Johnson, A.R. *Sacral Kinship in Ancient Israel*, Wales University Press, 2nd edition, 1967.
Mowinckel, S. *He That Cometh*, Blackwell, 1959.

DEAD SEA SCROLLS
Burrows, M. *The Dead Sea Scrolls*, Secker and Warburg, 1955. *More Light on the Dead Sea Scrolls*, Secker and Warburg, 1958.
Gaster, T.H. *The Scriptures of the Dead Sea Scrolls*, Secker and Warburg, 1957.

Index